STEW

THE AUSTRALIAN
Women's Weekly

STEW

braises & casseroles

acp
books

contents

Start with a pot and a lid, some herbs, a few vegies and a bit of meat and you'll be on your way to that sensational slow-cooked meal aroma. Stews and casseroles mean melt-in-your-mouth meat or fish, and delicious, warm sauce to dip your bread into. Truly comfort food, they are an economical way to feed a crowd. You can get a big batch going over the weekend and freeze in single servings for a brilliant last-minute weekday meal. Stews can be cooked on top of the stove or in the oven – or a bit of both. There is only one rule-of-thumb – give it time. Generally speaking, a stew should bubble away slowly for a good, long cook, and is often even better when heated up again the next day. This allows the delicate flavours to develop. Coating meat in flour and browning it before adding other ingredients will help thicken the sauce. Make sure the lid fits the dish tightly and use a heat-spreading mat, available from supermarkets, when cooking on the stove for an even distribution of heat. At serving time, add a generous spoonful of mash, polenta, couscous or one of our many other on-the-side suggestions and you've got a delicious, hearty meal.

poultry

Italian white bean and chicken stew

1 cup (200g) dried cannellini beans
1kg chicken thigh fillets, chopped coarsely
¼ cup finely chopped fresh oregano
1 tablespoon olive oil
1 medium fennel bulb (300g)
2 medium brown onions (300g), sliced thinly
2 cloves garlic, crushed
6 medium tomatoes (900g), peeled, seeded, chopped coarsely
3 large zucchini (450g), chopped coarsely
½ cup coarsely chopped fresh basil

1 Cover beans with cold water in medium bowl; stand overnight. Drain; rinse under cold water. Place beans in medium saucepan of boiling water; return to the boil. Reduce heat; simmer, uncovered, about 30 minutes or until beans are almost tender. Drain.
2 Meanwhile, combine chicken and oregano in medium bowl. Heat oil in large saucepan; cook chicken, in batches, until browned.
3 Trim then slice fennel thinly. Coarsely chop enough fennel fronds to make 2 tablespoons; reserve.
4 Cook onion, garlic and sliced fennel in same dish, stirring, until vegetables just soften. Return chicken to dish with tomato, zucchini and beans; cook, covered, over low heat, about 15 minutes or until chicken is cooked through. Uncover; simmer 5 minutes.
5 Remove stew from heat; stir in basil and reserved fronds. Serve with a loaf of french bread, if desired.

preparation time 35 minutes (plus standing time)
cooking time 35 minutes **serves** 4
nutritional count per serving 23.3g total fat (6.2g saturated fat); 2119kJ (507 cal); 16.2g carbohydrate; 54.5g protein; 9.0g fibre

Butter chicken

1 tablespoon garam masala
1 teaspoon chilli powder
2 cloves garlic, chopped coarsely
4cm piece fresh ginger (20g), grated
2 tablespoons lemon juice
⅓ cup (90g) tomato paste
1 cup (150g) roasted, unsalted cashews
¼ cup (60ml) buttermilk
800g chicken thigh fillets, chopped coarsely
40g butter
1 large brown onion (200g), sliced thinly
1 cinnamon stick
6 cardamom pods, bruised
425g can crushed tomatoes
¾ cup (180ml) chicken stock
¼ cup (60ml) buttermilk, extra
¼ cup loosely packed fresh coriander leaves

1 Dry-fry garam masala and chilli in small frying pan, stirring, until fragrant.
2 Blend or process chilli mixture with garlic, ginger, juice, paste, half of the nuts and half of the buttermilk until smooth. Combine nut mixture, remaining buttermilk and chicken in large bowl. Cover; refrigerate 3 hours or overnight.
3 Melt butter in large saucepan; cook onion, cinnamon and cardamom, stirring, until onion browns. Add undrained chicken mixture; cook, uncovered, 10 minutes, stirring occasionally.
4 Add undrained tomatoes and stock; bring to the boil. Reduce heat; simmer, uncovered, stirring occasionally, about 35 minutes or until chicken is cooked through and mixture thickens slightly. Remove from heat; stir in extra buttermilk.
5 Coarsely chop remaining nuts; top chicken with nuts and coriander. Serve with pilaf with almonds (see page 364), if desired.

preparation time 15 minutes (plus refrigeration time)
cooking time 1 hour **serves** 4
nutritional count per serving 42.3g total fat (13.5g saturated fat); 2709kJ (648 cal); 17.5g carbohydrate; 48.0g protein; 5.5g fibre

Braised spatchcocks with spinach

3 x 500g spatchcocks
1 medium leek (350g), chopped coarsely
2 cloves garlic, crushed
1 medium brown onion (150g), chopped coarsely
4 rindless bacon rashers (260g), chopped finely
½ cup (125ml) dry white wine
1 cup (250ml) chicken stock
2 bay leaves
300g brussels sprouts, halved
500g spinach, trimmed, chopped coarsely
½ cup coarsely chopped fresh mint

1 Cut along both sides of spatchcocks' backbones; discard backbones.
Cut each spatchcock into four pieces. Rinse under cold water; pat dry
with absorbent paper.
2 Cook spatchcock, in batches, in large oiled saucepan until browned
lightly both sides.
3 Cook leek, garlic, onion and bacon in same pan, stirring, 5 minutes or
until leek softens. Add wine, stock and bay leaves; bring to the boil. Return
spatchcocks with any juices to pan, reduce heat; simmer, uncovered,
about 20 minutes or until liquid has almost evaporated. Discard bay
leaves. Remove spatchcock from pan; cover to keep warm.
4 Add sprouts to pan; simmer, uncovered, about 3 minutes or until tender.
Stir in spinach and mint; cook until spinach just wilts.
5 Serve spatchcock with sprouts and spinach mixture.

preparation time 30 minutes   **cooking time** 40 minutes
serves 4
nutritional count per serving 30.1g total fat (9.6g saturated fat);
2304kJ (551 cal); 7.4g carbohydrate; 57.6g protein; 7.3g fibre

Clay pot chicken

800g chicken thigh fillets, halved
4 cloves garlic, crushed
1 tablespoon fish sauce
1 tablespoon soy sauce
1 tablespoon hoisin sauce
2 tablespoons lime juice
10cm stick fresh lemon grass (20g), chopped finely
1 large brown onion (200g), quartered
1 fresh long red chilli, sliced thinly
½ cup (125ml) chicken stock
100g fresh shiitake mushrooms, halved
4 green onions, cut into 4cm pieces
½ small cabbage (600g), cut into 6cm squares

1 Combine chicken, garlic, sauces, juice and lemon grass in large bowl.
Cover; refrigerate 3 hours or overnight.
2 Preheat oven to 180°C/160°C fan-forced.
3 Place chicken mixture in clay pot or 2.5-litre (10-cup) ovenproof dish
with brown onion, chilli and stock; mix gently to combine. Cook, covered,
in oven 45 minutes. Add mushroom, green onion and cabbage; cook,
covered, stirring occasionally, about 15 minutes or until chicken is
cooked through.

preparation time 10 minutes (plus refrigeration time)
cooking time 1 hour **serves** 4
nutritional count per serving 9.2g total fat (2.5g saturated fat);
1296kJ (310 cal); 9.4g carbohydrate; 46.6g protein; 8.2g fibre

Coconut chicken masala

2 tablespoons peanut oil
1 large brown onion (200g), sliced thinly
2 cloves garlic, crushed
1 tablespoon coriander seeds
1 tablespoon ground cumin
1 teaspoon ground turmeric
1 teaspoon ground ginger
1 teaspoon garam masala
½ teaspoon ground cardamom
2 teaspoons chilli powder
1 teaspoon coarsely ground black pepper
1.5kg chicken breast fillets, chopped coarsely
¼ cup (70g) tomato paste
1½ cups (375ml) chicken stock
½ cup (125ml) water
1 teaspoon cornflour
¾ cup (180ml) coconut cream
2 tablespoons coarsely chopped fresh coriander

1 Heat oil in large saucepan; cook onion and garlic, stirring, until onion softens. Add coriander seeds; cook, stirring, about 1 minute or until seeds start to pop. Add remaining spices; cook, stirring, until mixture is fragrant.
2 Add chicken to pan, turning to coat pieces in spice mixture; cook, stirring, until chicken is just browned.
3 Stir in tomato paste, stock and the water; bring to the boil. Reduce heat; simmer, covered, about 20 minutes or until chicken is cooked through.
4 Stir blended cornflour and coconut cream into chicken curry. Bring to the boil; cook, stirring, until mixture boils and thickens. Stir in fresh coriander just before serving.

preparation time 10 minutes **cooking time** 35 minutes
serves 4
nutritional count per serving 27.6g total fat (12.3g saturated fat); 2663kJ (637 cal); 7.7g carbohydrate; 88.1g protein; 2.5g fibre

Braised sweet ginger duck

2kg duck
½ cup (125ml) chinese cooking wine
⅓ cup (80ml) soy sauce
¼ cup (55g) firmly packed brown sugar
1 whole star anise
3 green onions, halved
3 cloves garlic, quartered
10cm piece fresh ginger (50g), unpeeled, chopped coarsely
3 cups (750ml) water
2 teaspoons sea salt
1 teaspoon five-spice powder
800g baby buk choy, halved

1 Preheat oven to 180°C/160°C fan-forced.
2 Discard neck from duck, wash duck; pat dry with absorbent paper. Score duck in thickest parts of skin; cut duck in half through breastbone and along both sides of backbone, discard backbone. Tuck wings under duck.
3 Place duck, skin-side down, in medium shallow baking dish; add combined wine, sauce, sugar, star anise, onion, garlic, ginger and the water. Cook, covered, in oven about 1 hour or until duck is cooked as desired.
4 Increase oven temperature to 220°C/200°C fan-forced. Remove duck from braising liquid; strain liquid through muslin-lined sieve into large saucepan. Return duck, skin-side up, to wire rack in dish. Rub combined salt and five-spice all over duck; roast duck, uncovered, in oven about 30 minutes or until skin is crisp.
5 Skim fat from surface of braising liquid; bring to the boil. Reduce heat; simmer, uncovered, 10 minutes. Add buk choy; simmer, covered, about 5 minutes or until buk choy is just tender.
6 Cut duck halves into two pieces; divide buk choy, braising liquid and duck among plates. Serve with steamed jasmine rice, if desired.

preparation time 20 minutes **cooking time** 1 hour 50 minutes
serves 4
nutritional count per serving 105.7g total fat (31.7g saturated fat); 4974kJ (1190 cal); 17.9g carbohydrate; 40.8g protein; 3.5g fibre

Chicken tagine with dates and honey

1kg chicken thigh fillets
2 tablespoons olive oil
2 medium brown onions (300g), sliced thinly
4 cloves garlic, crushed
1 teaspoon cumin seeds
1 teaspoon ground coriander
1 teaspoon ground ginger
1 teaspoon ground turmeric
1 teaspoon ground cinnamon
½ teaspoon chilli powder
¼ teaspoon ground nutmeg
1½ cups (375ml) chicken stock
1 cup (250ml) water
½ cup (85g) seedless dates, halved
¼ cup (90g) honey
½ cup (80g) blanched almonds, roasted
1 tablespoon chopped fresh coriander

1 Cut chicken into 3cm strips. Heat half of the oil in medium saucepan; cook chicken, in batches, stirring, until browned. Drain on absorbent paper.
2 Heat remaining oil in same pan; cook onion, garlic and spices, stirring, until onion is soft.
3 Return chicken to pan with stock and the water; simmer, covered, 1 hour. Remove lid, simmer about 30 minutes or until mixture is thickened slightly and chicken is tender. Stir in dates, honey and nuts; sprinkle with coriander.

preparation time 25 minutes **cooking time** 1 hour 45 minutes
serves 4
nutritional count per serving 38.7g total fat (7.7g saturated fat); 2888kJ (691 cal); 31.2g carbohydrate; 53.1g protein; 4.2g fibre

Chicken cacciatore with split pea salad

1 cup (200g) green split peas
2 tablespoons olive oil
1.5kg chicken pieces, skin on
1 medium brown onion (150g), chopped finely
½ cup (125ml) dry white wine
2 tablespoons white wine vinegar
½ cup (125ml) chicken stock
410g can crushed tomatoes
¼ cup (70g) tomato paste
½ cup (60g) seeded black olives, chopped coarsely
2 tablespoons drained capers, rinsed, chopped coarsely
2 cloves garlic, crushed
½ cup coarsely chopped fresh flat-leaf parsley
½ cup coarsely chopped fresh basil

1 Place peas in medium bowl, cover with cold water; stand overnight, drain. Rinse under cold water; drain.
2 Heat half of the oil in large deep saucepan; cook chicken, in batches, until browned all over.
3 Cook onion in same pan, stirring, until onion softens. Stir in wine, vinegar, stock, undrained tomatoes and paste.
4 Return chicken to pan, fitting pieces upright and tightly together in single layer; bring to the boil. Reduce heat; simmer, covered, 1 hour. Uncover; simmer about 45 minutes or until chicken is tender. Skim fat from surface; stir in olives.
5 Meanwhile, place peas in large saucepan of boiling water; return to the boil. Reduce heat; simmer, uncovered, about 40 minutes or until peas are tender, drain.
6 Combine peas, capers, garlic, herbs and remaining oil in large bowl. Serve chicken cacciatore with split pea salad.

preparation time 20 minutes (plus standing time)
cooking time 2 hours 10 minutes **serves** 4
nutritional count per serving 37.2g total fat (9.7g saturated fat); 2830kJ (677 cal); 34.1g carbohydrate; 47.0g protein; 8.5g fibre

Spicy caribbean-style chicken stew

1kg chicken thigh fillets
2 teaspoons ground allspice
1 teaspoon ground cinnamon
pinch ground nutmeg
1 tablespoon finely chopped fresh thyme
¼ cup (60ml) olive oil
2 medium brown onions (300g), sliced thinly
2 cloves garlic, crushed
1 tablespoon grated fresh ginger
1 teaspoon sambal oelek   *illes 1 Vinegar*
5 medium tomatoes (650g), peeled, seeded, chopped finely
2 tablespoons brown sugar
2 teaspoons grated orange rind
2 tablespoons soy sauce
1 medium kumara (400g), chopped coarsely
2 fresh corn cobs, sliced thickly
125g baby spinach leaves

1 Cut chicken into 2cm strips. Toss chicken in combined spices and thyme.
2 Heat half of the oil in large saucepan; cook chicken, in batches, stirring, until browned. Drain on absorbent paper.
3 Heat remaining oil in pan; cook onion, garlic, ginger and sambal oelek, stirring, until onion is soft.
4 Add tomato, sugar, rind, sauce, kumara, corn and chicken; cook, covered, about 15 minutes or until chicken and vegetables are tender. Remove cover; simmer 5 minutes.
5 Remove from heat. Add spinach; stir until spinach is wilted.

preparation time 45 minutes **cooking time** 50 minutes
serves 6
nutritional count per serving 22.3g total fat (5.0g saturated fat); 2015kJ (482 cal); 29.7g carbohydrate; 37.5g protein; 6.7g fibre

Chicken with tomatoes and green olives

1 tablespoon olive oil
4 chicken thigh fillets (880g)
4 chicken drumsticks (600g)
½ cup (125ml) dry white wine
8 cloves garlic, peeled
1 tablespoon finely chopped fresh lemon thyme
3 bay leaves
100g semi-dried tomatoes
1½ cups (375ml) chicken stock
2 teaspoons cornflour
1 tablespoon water
⅓ cup (50g) seeded green olives

1 Heat oil in large heavy-based frying pan; cook chicken until lightly browned all over.
2 Add wine to pan; bring to the boil. Add garlic, thyme, bay leaves, tomatoes and stock; simmer, covered, about 15 minutes or until chicken is cooked through. Remove chicken from pan; cover to keep warm.
3 Add blended cornflour and water to pan; stir until mixture boils and thickens slightly.
4 Return chicken to pan with olives; simmer until heated through. Discard bay leaves before serving.

preparation time 10 minutes **cooking time** 30 minutes
serves 4
nutritional count per serving 32.7g total fat (9.1g saturated fat); 2617kJ (626 cal); 14.1g carbohydrate; 62.0g protein; 4.8g fibre

Braised spatchcock with fennel and ouzo

¼ cup (60ml) olive oil
4 x 500g spatchcocks
1 medium lemon (140g), quartered
2 large fennel bulbs (1kg), halved, sliced thinly
1 large brown onion (200g), sliced thinly
2 cloves garlic, sliced thinly
¼ cup (60ml) ouzo
2 cups (500ml) chicken stock
3 large zucchini (450g), sliced thinly
2 tablespoons lemon juice
½ cup (125ml) cream
2 tablespoons coarsely chopped fennel fronds

1 Preheat oven to 200°C/180°C fan-forced.
2 Heat 1 tablespoon of the oil in large deep flameproof baking dish; cook spatchcocks, one at a time, over heat, until browned all over. Place one lemon quarter in cavity of each spatchcock.
3 Heat remaining oil in same dish; cook fennel, onion and garlic, stirring, over heat until onion softens. Add ouzo; cook, stirring, until ouzo evaporates. Add stock; bring to the boil. Place spatchcocks on fennel mixture; cook, uncovered, in oven about 35 minutes or until spatchcocks are just cooked through.
4 Add zucchini to dish, submerging into fennel mixture; cook, uncovered, in oven about 5 minutes or until zucchini is tender. Transfer spatchcocks to large plate; cover to keep warm.
5 Bring fennel mixture to the boil. Add juice and cream; return to the boil. Reduce heat; simmer, uncovered, 5 minutes. Stir in half of the fennel fronds.
6 Using slotted spoon, divide fennel mixture among plates; top with spatchcock. Drizzle with pan juices; sprinkle with remaining fennel fronds, serve with risoni, if desired.

preparation time 30 minutes **cooking time** 1 hour 10 minutes
serves 4
nutritional count per serving 61.4g total fat (20.8g saturated fat); 3407kJ (815 cal); 10.0g carbohydrate; 49.1g protein; 6.4g fibre

Chicken stuffed with ricotta, basil and prosciutto

8 chicken thigh cutlets (1.3kg)
⅔ cup (130g) ricotta cheese
4 slices prosciutto (60g), halved lengthways
8 large fresh basil leaves
1 tablespoon olive oil
1 medium brown onion (150g), chopped finely
2 cloves garlic, chopped finely
1 medium carrot (120g), chopped finely
1 trimmed celery stalk (100g), chopped finely
2 tablespoons tomato paste
½ cup (125ml) dry white wine
8 small tomatoes (720g), peeled, chopped coarsely
425g can diced tomatoes
½ cup (125ml) water

1 Preheat oven to 160°C/140°C fan-forced.
2 Using small sharp knife, cut a pocket through thickest part of each cutlet over the bone, push 1 tablespoon of the cheese, one slice of prosciutto and one basil leaf into each pocket; secure pocket closed with toothpick.
3 Heat oil in large deep flameproof baking dish; cook chicken, in batches, until browned all over.
4 Cook onion, garlic, carrot and celery in same dish, stirring, about 5 minutes or until onion softens. Add paste; cook, stirring, 2 minutes. Add wine; bring to the boil. Reduce heat; simmer, uncovered, 1 minute. Add chopped fresh tomato, undrained canned tomato and the water; bring to the boil. Reduce heat; simmer, uncovered, 10 minutes.
5 Return chicken to dish, cover; cook in oven 1 hour. Remove lid; cook a further 20 minutes or until chicken is cooked through. Remove toothpicks; serve chicken with extra basil leaves and sourdough, if desired.

preparation time 30 minutes **cooking time** 2 hours
serves 4
nutritional count per serving 46.8g total fat (15.5g saturated fat); 2922kJ (699 cal); 11.2g carbohydrate; 53.3g protein; 5.5g fibre

Chicken with rosemary and garlic

8 chicken thigh cutlets (1.3kg), skin on
2 tablespoons plain flour
2 teaspoons sweet paprika
1 teaspoon cracked black pepper
1 tablespoon olive oil
4 cloves garlic, unpeeled
2 stalks fresh rosemary
1½ cups (375ml) chicken stock
½ cup (125ml) dry white wine

1 Preheat oven to 180°C/160°C fan-forced.
2 Toss chicken in combined flour, paprika and pepper; shake away excess flour mixture from chicken.
3 Heat oil in large flameproof baking dish; cook chicken, in batches, until browned all over.
4 Return all chicken to same dish with garlic, rosemary, stock and wine; bring to the boil. Transfer dish to oven; cook, uncovered, about 40 minutes or until chicken is tender and cooked through.
5 Remove chicken from dish; cover to keep warm. Cook pan juices in same dish over medium heat, uncovered, about 5 minutes or until sauce thickens slightly.
6 Divide chicken among serving plates, drizzle with sauce. Serve with steamed sugar snap peas, if desired.

preparation time 20 minutes **cooking time** 55 minutes
serves 4
nutritional count per serving 40.1g total fat (12.4g saturated fat); 2433kJ (582 cal); 5.5g carbohydrate; 43.1g protein; 1.4g fibre

Chicken fricassee

40g butter
8 shallots (200g), peeled
20 baby carrots (400g), halved
1kg chicken thigh fillets, cut into thirds
2 tablespoons plain flour
½ cup (125ml) dry white wine
1½ cups (375g) chicken stock
2 tablespoons dijon mustard
2 large kumara (1kg), chopped coarsely
20g butter, extra
½ cup (125ml) cream
2 egg yolks
¼ cup (60ml) cream, extra
1 tablespoon lemon juice
2 tablespoons coarsely chopped fresh tarragon

1 Heat butter in large heavy-based saucepan; cook shallots and carrots, over low heat, stirring occasionally, about 5 minutes or until browned lightly. Remove from pan.
2 Cook chicken, in batches, in same pan, over low heat, until browned lightly.
3 Add flour to pan; cook, stirring, until mixture bubbles and thickens. Gradually stir in combined wine, stock and mustard. Return chicken to pan with shallots and carrots; bring to the boil. Reduce heat; simmer, covered, about 45 minutes or until chicken is cooked through.
4 Meanwhile, boil, steam or microwave kumara until tender; drain. Mash kumara with extra butter and cream in large bowl until smooth. Cover to keep warm.
5 Combine egg yolks, extra cream, juice and tarragon in medium jug. Remove fricassee from heat. Gradually add cream mixture, stirring constantly. Serve with kumara mash.

preparation time 20 minutes **cooking time** 1 hour 10 minutes
serves 4
nutritional count per serving 54.1g total fat (27.9g saturated fat); 3825kJ (915 cal); 43.5g carbohydrate; 56.4g protein; 7.6g fibre

Spanish chicken casserole

1 tablespoon olive oil
4 chicken drumsticks (600g)
4 chicken thigh cutlets (800g)
1 large brown onion (200g), chopped finely
4 medium potatoes (800g), quartered
½ cup (80g) roasted pine nuts
½ cup (80g) roasted blanched almonds
3 cups (750ml) chicken stock
1 cup (250ml) dry white wine
⅓ cup (80ml) lemon juice
4 cloves garlic, crushed
2 tablespoons fresh thyme leaves
½ cup coarsely chopped fresh flat-leaf parsley
500g baby green beans, trimmed

1 Preheat oven to 180°C/160°C fan-forced.
2 Heat oil in large flameproof casserole dish; cook chicken, in batches, over heat until browned.
3 Cook onion in same dish, stirring over heat, until soft. Return chicken to dish with potato, nuts, stock, wine, juice, garlic, thyme and half of the parsley; bring to the boil. Cover; cook in oven about 1 hour or until chicken is cooked through.
4 Meanwhile, boil, steam or microwave beans until tender; drain.
5 Serve chicken with beans; sprinkle with remaining parsley.

preparation time 10 minutes **cooking time** 1 hour 25 minutes
serves 4
nutritional count per serving 61.4g total fat (12.4g saturated fat);
4050kJ (969 cal); 35.0g carbohydrate; 57.0g protein; 10.4g fibre

Chicken donburi

4 dried shiitake mushrooms
½ teaspoon dashi powder
1 cup (250ml) boiling water
1 tablespoon vegetable oil
4 medium brown onions (600g), sliced thinly
1½ cups (300g) koshihikari rice
3 cups (750ml) cold water
¼ cup (60ml) soy sauce
2 tablespoons mirin
1 teaspoon white sugar
600g chicken breast fillets, chopped coarsely
4 eggs, beaten lightly
2 green onions, sliced thinly

1 Place mushrooms in small heatproof bowl, cover with boiling water, stand 20 minutes; drain. Discard stems; slice caps thinly.
2 Meanwhile, combine dashi with the boiling water in small jug.
3 Heat oil in a large frying pan; cook brown onion, stirring, 10 minutes or until browned lightly. Add half of the dashi mixture, reduce heat; simmer, stirring occasionally, about 10 minutes or until softened. Transfer to medium bowl.
4 Bring rice and the cold water to the boil in large saucepan, uncovered, stirring occasionally. Reduce heat to as low as possible; cover with a tight-fitting lid, cook rice 12 minutes. Do not remove lid or stir rice during cooking time. Remove from heat; stand, covered, 10 minutes.
5 Meanwhile, combine remaining dashi mixture with sauce, mirin and sugar in same frying pan; bring to the boil. Add chicken and mushroom; cook, covered, about 5 minutes or until chicken is cooked through.
6 Combine egg with cooked onion in bowl, pour over chicken mixture; cook, covered, over low heat, about 5 minutes or until egg just sets.
7 Divide rice among serving bowls; top with chicken mixture, sprinkle with green onion.

preparation time 20 minutes (plus standing time)
cooking time 40 minutes **serves** 4
nutritional count per serving 13.8g total fat (3.2g saturated fat);
2567kJ (614 cal); 69.5g carbohydrate; 48.8g protein; 2.9g fibre

Chicken in yogurt

2 teaspoons ground cumin
2 teaspoons ground cardamom
1 teaspoon ground cinnamon
½ teaspoon ground clove
½ teaspoon ground turmeric
½ cup (80g) blanched almonds
2cm piece fresh ginger (10g), chopped coarsely
2 cloves garlic, quartered
500g yogurt
8 chicken thigh cutlets (1.6kg), skin removed
2 tablespoons vegetable oil
2 medium brown onions (300g), sliced thinly
⅓ cup (80ml) lemon juice
¼ cup finely chopped fresh coriander

1 Dry-fry spices and nuts in small heated frying pan, stirring, until nuts are browned lightly.
2 Blend or process nut mixture with ginger and garlic until mixture forms a paste. Combine mixture with yogurt in large bowl, add chicken; mix well. Cover; refrigerate 3 hours or overnight.
3 Heat oil in large saucepan; cook onion, stirring, until soft. Add chicken mixture; simmer, covered, about 45 minutes or until chicken is cooked through. Stir in juice.
4 Serve curry sprinkled with coriander.

preparation time 30 minutes (plus refrigeration time)
cooking time 1 hour **serves** 4
nutritional count per serving 64.8g total fat (17.8g saturated fat); 3586kJ (858 cal); 10.4g carbohydrate; 58.1g protein; 3.2g fibre

Quince and chicken tagine

2 medium quinces (700g), peeled, cored, cut into wedges
40g butter
⅓ cup (115g) honey
3 cups (750ml) water
2 teaspoons orange flower water
2 teaspoons olive oil
4 chicken drumsticks (600g)
4 chicken thigh cutlets (800g), skin removed
1 large brown onion (200g), chopped coarsely
3 cloves garlic, crushed
1 teaspoon ground cumin
1 teaspoon ground ginger
pinch saffron threads
2 cups (500ml) chicken stock
2 large zucchini (300g), chopped coarsely
¼ cup coarsely chopped fresh coriander

1 Place quinces, butter, honey, the water and orange flower water in medium saucepan; bring to the boil. Reduce heat; simmer, covered, 1 hour, stirring occasionally. Remove lid, cook, stirring occasionally, about 45 minutes or until quince is red in colour.
2 Meanwhile, heat oil in large frying pan; cook chicken, in batches, until browned.
3 Cook onion, garlic and spices in same pan, stirring, until onion softens. Return chicken to pan then add stock; bring to the boil. Reduce heat; simmer, covered, 20 minutes. Remove lid; simmer, about 20 minutes or until chicken is cooked though. Add zucchini; cook, uncovered, about 10 minutes or until zucchini is tender. Stir in quince and ½ cup of the quince syrup.
4 Divide tagine among serving plates; sprinkle with coriander. Serve with spinach couscous (see page 347), if desired.

preparation time 20 minutes **cooking time** 1 hour 40 minutes
serves 4
nutritional count per serving 32.1g total fat (12.2g saturated fat); 2780kJ (665 cal); 42.1g carbohydrate; 46.7g protein; 11.4g fibre

Spanish-style chicken

2 teaspoons olive oil
1 large brown onion (200g), chopped coarsely
2 cloves garlic, crushed
2 medium green capsicums (400g), chopped coarsely
16 chicken drumettes (2kg)
410g can tomato puree
1 teaspoon hot paprika
1 tablespoon ground coriander
1 tablespoon ground cumin
½ teaspoon cayenne pepper
2 cups (320g) fresh corn kernels
½ cup (125ml) dry red wine
1 cup (250ml) chicken stock
2 bay leaves
1½ cups (300g) long-grain white rice
2 tablespoons finely chopped fresh flat-leaf parsley

1 Preheat oven to 200°C/180°C fan-forced.
2 Heat oil in large flameproof baking dish with tight-fitting lid; cook onion, garlic and capsicum, stirring over heat, until vegetables just soften. Remove vegetables, leaving as much oil in dish as possible. Add chicken, in batches, to dish; cook until browned all over.
3 Return chicken and vegetables to dish with tomato puree, spices, corn, wine, stock, bay leaves and rice; bring to the boil. Cover tightly; cook in oven about 30 minutes or until rice is tender and chicken cooked through. Sprinkle with parsley just before serving.

preparation time 20 minutes **cooking time** 45 minutes
serves 8
nutritional count per serving 17.1g total fat (4.8g saturated fat); 1919kJ (459 cal); 41.4g carbohydrate; 30.2g protein; 3.9g fibre

Braised spatchcock with peas and lettuce

3 x 500g spatchcocks
1 medium leek (350g)
2 bay leaves
1 sprig fresh thyme
1 sprig fresh rosemary
4 fresh flat-leaf parsley stalks
50g butter
2 cloves garlic, crushed
1 large brown onion (200g), chopped finely
8 rindless bacon rashers (520g), chopped coarsely
¼ cup (35g) plain flour
1½ cups (375ml) dry white wine
3 cups (750ml) chicken stock
500g frozen peas
1 large butter lettuce, shredded finely
½ cup coarsely chopped fresh mint

1 Cut along both sides of spatchcocks' backbones; discard backbones. Cut in half between breasts. Rinse spatchcock halves under cold water; pat dry with absorbent paper.
2 Cut leek in half crossways; chop white bottom half finely, reserve. Using kitchen string, tie green top half of leek, bay leaves, thyme, rosemary and parsley stalks into a bundle.
3 Heat butter in large saucepan; cook spatchcock, in batches, until browned lightly both sides. Cook reserved chopped leek, garlic, onion and bacon in same pan, stirring, about 10 minutes or until onion softens. Add flour; cook, stirring, 2 minutes. Gradually add wine and stock; bring to the boil, stirring constantly until mixture boils and thickens. Return spatchcock to pan with herb bundle, reduce heat; simmer, covered, 30 minutes.
4 Discard herb bundle. Add peas, lettuce and mint to pan; simmer, uncovered, about 5 minutes or until peas are just tender. Serve with mashed potato (see page 360), if desired.

preparation time 30 minutes **cooking time** 55 minutes
serves 6
nutritional count per serving 39.3g total fat (15.2g saturated fat); 2767kJ (662 cal); 14.2g carbohydrate; 49.9g protein; 7.6g fibre

Chicken with prunes and honey

1.5kg chicken
¼ cup (60ml) olive oil
1 medium brown onion (150g), sliced thinly
1 teaspoon ground cinnamon
pinch saffron threads
¼ teaspoon ground turmeric
2 teaspoons ground ginger
1¼ cups (310ml) water
⅓ cup (120g) honey
¾ cup (120g) seeded prunes
3 teaspoons sesame seeds
30g butter
½ cup (80g) blanched almonds
1 tablespoon thinly sliced preserved lemon rind

1 Halve chicken lengthways. Cut each half crossways through the centre; separate breasts from wings and thighs from legs. You will have eight pieces.
2 Heat oil in large deep frying pan; cook chicken, in batches, until well browned all over. Drain all but 1 tablespoon of the oil from pan.
3 Cook onion in same pan, stirring, until soft. Add spices; cook, stirring, until fragrant. Return chicken to pan; stir to coat chicken in onion mixture. Add the water; bring to the boil. Reduce heat; simmer, covered, about 30 minutes or until chicken is tender.
4 Remove chicken from pan; cover to keep warm. Add honey and prunes to pan; simmer, uncovered, about 15 minutes or until sauce thickens slightly.
5 Meanwhile, toast sesame seeds in small saucepan, stirring, until lightly browned. Remove from pan immediately.
6 Melt butter in same saucepan; cook almonds, stirring, until almonds are lightly browned. Remove from pan immediately.
7 Return chicken to frying pan; stir over heat until chicken is heated through. Divide chicken and sauce among serving plates; sprinkle with seeds, nuts and preserved lemon.

preparation time 20 minutes **cooking time** 1 hour
serves 4
nutritional count per serving 62.3g total fat (16.2g saturated fat); 3712kJ (888 cal); 37.5g carbohydrate; 43.3g protein; 5.0g fibre

Chicken, leek and bacon casserole

4 chicken thigh cutlets (800g), skin on
¼ cup (35g) plain flour
1 tablespoon olive oil
2 stalks fresh rosemary
3 cloves garlic, unpeeled
½ cup (125ml) dry white wine
¾ cup (180ml) chicken stock
20g butter
4 rindless bacon rashers (260g), chopped coarsely
2 small leeks (400g), sliced
1 trimmed stick celery (100g), sliced thinly
2 sprigs fresh thyme
2 tablespoons plain flour
½ cup (125ml) dry white wine
1 cup (250ml) water
1 bunch baby carrots (400g), trimmed

1 Preheat oven to 180°C/160°C fan-forced.
2 Toss chicken in flour; shake away excess flour.
3 Heat oil in large flameproof baking dish; cook chicken until browned all over. Add rosemary, garlic, wine and stock; bring to the boil. Cover dish, cook in oven about 40 minutes or until chicken is cooked through. Strain pan juices and reserve.
4 Squeeze the garlic from skins, mash until smooth.
5 Melt the butter in a large saucepan; cook bacon, leek, celery and thyme, stirring, until bacon is crisp and leek is soft.
6 Add flour, cook, stirring, 1 minute. Gradually stir in wine; bring to the boil. Add garlic, reserved pan juices and water; bring to the boil. Add carrots and chicken; simmer, uncovered, 20 minutes or until carrots are tender and sauce is thickened.
7 Serve casserole with mashed potato (see page 360), if desired.

preparation time 25 minutes **cooking time** 1 hour 20 minutes
serves 4
nutritional count per serving 38.1g total fat (13.2g saturated fat); 2621kJ (627 cal); 18.6g carbohydrate; 40.3g protein; 5.6g fibre

Coq à la bière

1.4kg chicken
¼ cup (35g) plain flour
20g butter
2 large carrots (360g)
1 tablespoon olive oil
6 shallots (150g), peeled
2 tablespoons brandy
1½ cups (375ml) pale ale
1 cup (250ml) chicken stock
1 bay leaf
2 sprigs fresh thyme
2 sprigs fresh flat-leaf parsley
20g butter, extra
200g mushrooms
½ cup (125ml) cream

1 Halve chicken lengthways; cut halves crossways through the centre.
Separate breasts from wings; separate thighs from legs.
2 Coat chicken pieces in flour; shake off excess. Melt butter in large
saucepan; cook chicken, in batches, until browned all over.
3 Meanwhile, cut carrots into 5cm lengths; cut lengths in half lengthways
then cut halves thickly into strips.
4 Heat oil in same cleaned pan; cook shallots, stirring occasionally,
about 5 minutes or until browned lightly. Add carrot; cook, stirring,
5 minutes. Add brandy; cook, stirring, until liquid evaporates. Add
chicken, ale, stock and herbs; bring to the boil. Reduce heat; simmer,
uncovered, 1¼ hours.
5 Melt extra butter in medium frying pan; cook mushrooms, stirring,
until just tender. Add mushrooms and cream to chicken; cook, covered,
15 minutes. Serve with mashed potato (see page 360), if desired.

preparation time 30 minutes **cooking time** 1 hour 50 minutes
serves 4
nutritional count per serving 55.0g total fat (23.9g saturated fat);
3168kJ (758 cal); 13.5g carbohydrate; 40.1g protein; 3.9g fibre

Chicken cassoulet

1 cup (200g) dried haricot beans
500g spicy italian sausages
250g pork sausages
4 chicken thighs (900g)
4 chicken breasts on the bone (1kg)
1 tablespoon vegetable oil
3 rindless bacon rashers (195g), sliced thinly
2 cloves garlic, crushed
3 cloves
12 black peppercorns
1 trimmed stick celery (75g), cut into 5cm lengths
4 medium carrots (480g), sliced thinly
5 baby onions (125g), halved
½ cup (125ml) dry white wine
3 cups (750ml) water
2 tablespoons tomato paste

1 Place beans in large bowl; cover well with cold water. Cover; stand overnight. Drain.
2 Preheat oven to 180°C/160°C fan-forced.
3 Cook sausages in large saucepan of boiling water, uncovered, 2 minutes; drain.
4 Remove skin from chicken; cut breasts in half.
5 Heat oil in 5 litre (20-cup) flameproof casserole dish; cook chicken and sausages, in batches, until browned. Drain on absorbent paper; slice sausages thickly.
6 Add bacon to dish; cook, stirring, until crisp. Drain on absorbent paper.
7 Return chicken to dish with drained beans, garlic, spices, vegetables, wine, the water and tomato paste. Cook, covered, in oven 1½ hours.
8 Add sausages; cover. Cook about 30 minutes or until sausages are cooked. Serve sprinkled with bacon.

preparation time 25 minutes (plus standing time)
cooking time 2 hours 30 minutes
serves 8
nutritional count per serving 41.8g total fat (14.1g saturated fat); 3026kJ (724 cal); 16.5g carbohydrate; 64.9g protein; 7.6g fibre

Chicken drumettes
with roasted capsicum sauce

3 large red capsicums (1kg)
1 teaspoon ground cinnamon
½ teaspoon ground cumin
1 teaspoon cracked black pepper
1 tablespoon plain flour
1kg chicken drumettes
¼ cup (60ml) olive oil
1 large brown onion (200g), chopped finely
3 cloves garlic, crushed
1 large tomato (220g), chopped coarsely
1 cup (250ml) chicken stock

1 Quarter capsicums; discard seeds and membranes. Roast under grill or in very hot oven, skin-side up, until skin blisters and blackens. Cover capsicum pieces with plastic wrap or paper for 5 minutes; peel away skin then chop capsicum coarsely.
2 Meanwhile, combine cinnamon, cumin, pepper and flour in large bowl. Add chicken; toss to coat in mixture, shake off excess.
3 Heat 2 tablespoons of the oil in large deep frying pan; cook chicken, in batches, until browned all over.
4 Heat remaining oil in same pan; cook onion and garlic, stirring, until onion softens. Add capsicum, tomato and stock; bring to the boil. Return chicken to pan, reduce heat; simmer, covered, about 30 minutes or until chicken is cooked through.
5 Remove chicken from pan; blend or process sauce until smooth.
6 Serve chicken topped with capsicum sauce; serve with pilaf with almonds (see page 364), if desired.

preparation time 20 minutes **cooking time** 1 hour
serves 4
nutritional count per serving 29.5g total fat (6.6g saturated fat); 1877kJ (449 cal); 14.8g carbohydrate; 29.7g protein; 4.2g fibre

Chicken and merguez cassoulet

Ask your butcher to halve the chicken thigh cutlets for you.

1½ cups (290g) lima beans
1 tablespoon vegetable oil
8 chicken thigh cutlets (1.3kg), halved
6 merguez sausages (480g)
1 large brown onion (200g), chopped coarsely
2 medium carrots (240g), diced into 1cm pieces
2 cloves garlic, chopped finely
4 sprigs fresh thyme
2 tablespoons tomato paste
1 teaspoon finely grated lemon rind
425g can diced tomatoes
1 cup (250ml) chicken stock
1 cup (250ml) water
2 cups (140g) fresh breadcrumbs

1 Place beans in medium bowl, cover with cold water; stand overnight, drain. Rinse under cold water; drain. Cook beans in large saucepan of boiling water, uncovered, 10 minutes; drain.
2 Heat oil in large flameproof casserole dish; cook chicken, in batches, until browned all over. Cook sausages, in batches, in same dish until browned all over. Drain on absorbent paper; halve sausages. Reserve 1 tablespoon of fat from dish; discard remainder.
3 Preheat oven to 160°C/140°C fan-forced.
4 Heat reserved fat in same dish; cook onion, carrot, garlic and thyme, stirring, until onion softens. Add paste; cook, stirring, 2 minutes. Return chicken to dish with drained beans, rind, undrained tomatoes, stock and the water; bring to the boil. Cover; cook in oven 40 minutes. Uncover; cook further 1¼ hours or until liquid is almost absorbed and beans are tender.
5 Preheat grill.
6 Sprinkle cassoulet with breadcrumbs; place under preheated grill until breadcrumbs are browned lightly. Serve with couscous, if desired.

preparation time 25 minutes (plus standing time)
cooking time 2 hours 45 minutes **serves** 6
nutritional count per serving 42.1g total fat (14.2g saturated fat); 3469kJ (830 cal); 46.1g carbohydrate; 60.6g protein; 12.7g fibre

Coq au vin

800g spring onions
¼ cup (60ml) olive oil
6 rindless bacon rashers (390g), cut into 3cm pieces
300g button mushrooms
2 cloves garlic, crushed
8 chicken thigh fillets (880g)
¼ cup (35g) plain flour
2 cups (500ml) dry red wine
1½ cups (375ml) chicken stock
2 tablespoons tomato paste
3 bay leaves
4 sprigs fresh thyme
2 sprigs fresh rosemary

1 Trim green ends from onions, leaving about 4cm of stem attached; trim roots.
2 Heat 1 tablespoon of the oil in large frying pan; cook onion, stirring, until browned all over, remove from pan. Add bacon, mushrooms and garlic to same pan; cook, stirring, until bacon is crisp, remove from pan.
3 Toss chicken in flour; shake off excess. Heat remaining oil in same pan. Cook chicken, in batches, until browned all over; drain on absorbent paper.
4 Return chicken to pan with onion, bacon and mushroom mixture, and remaining ingredients. Bring to the boil; simmer, uncovered, about 35 minutes or until chicken is tender and sauce has thickened slightly. Remove bay leaves before serving.

preparation time 30 minutes **cooking time** 55 minutes
serves 4
nutritional count per serving 43.6g total fat (11.8g saturated fat); 3428kJ (820 cal); 16.3g carbohydrate; 67.8g protein; 6.4g fibre

Chicken tagine

2 tablespoons olive oil
2kg chicken thigh fillets
3 teaspoons cumin seeds
3 teaspoons ground coriander
1 tablespoon smoked paprika
3 teaspoons ground cumin
4 cinnamon sticks
4 medium brown onions (600g), sliced thinly
8 cloves garlic, crushed
3 cups (750ml) chicken stock
1 cup (250ml) dry red wine
1 cup (170g) seeded prunes
½ cup (80g) roasted blanched almonds
¼ cup coarsely chopped fresh flat-leaf parsley

1 Heat half of the oil in large saucepan; cook chicken, in batches, until browned.
2 Meanwhile, dry-fry spices in small heated frying pan, stirring until fragrant.
3 Heat remaining oil in same saucepan; cook onion and garlic, stirring, until onion softens. Return chicken to pan with spices, stock and wine; bring to the boil. Reduce heat; simmer, covered, 40 minutes.
4 Stir in prunes; simmer, uncovered, about 20 minutes or until chicken is tender. Stir in nuts and parsley.

preparation time 20 minutes **cooking time** 1 hour 30 minutes
serves 8
nutritional count per serving 28.8g total fat (6.7g saturated fat); 2236kJ (535 cals); 13.5g carbohydrate; 51.4g protein; 4.1g fibre

Greek-style drumsticks with olives and artichokes

2 tablespoons olive oil
12 chicken drumsticks (1.8kg)
1 medium white onion (150g), chopped finely
3 cloves garlic, crushed
1 tablespoon finely grated lemon rind
1½ cups (375ml) chicken stock
½ cup (125ml) dry white wine
340g jar marinated artichokes, drained, quartered
500g risoni
2 tablespoons finely chopped fresh oregano
1 cup (150g) seeded kalamata olives
1 tablespoon finely grated lemon rind, extra
¼ cup (60ml) lemon juice

1 Heat half of the oil in large heavy-based saucepan; cook drumsticks, in batches, until browned all over.
2 Heat remaining oil in same pan; cook onion and garlic, stirring, until onion softens. Add rind, stock, wine and artichokes; bring to the boil. Return chicken to pan, reduce heat; simmer, covered, 20 minutes. Remove lid; simmer, about 10 minutes or until chicken is cooked through.
3 Meanwhile, cook risoni in large saucepan of boiling water, uncovered, until just tender; drain.
4 Remove chicken from pan; stir oregano, olives, extra juice and extra rind into sauce.
5 Serve chicken with sauce on risoni.

preparation time 15 minutes **cooking time** 1 hour
serves 4
nutritional count per serving 44.7g total fat (11.7g saturated fat); 4631kJ (1108 cal); 98.7g carbohydrate; 67.8g protein; 5.7g fibre

Mexican chicken stew

1 tablespoon vegetable oil
8 chicken drumsticks (1.2kg)
1 large red onion (300g), sliced thickly
2 cloves garlic, crushed
2 fresh long red chillies, chopped finely
1 teaspoon ground cumin
4 medium tomatoes (600g), chopped coarsely
1 cup (250ml) chicken stock
⅓ cup loosely packed fresh oregano leaves
420g can kidney beans, rinsed, drained
1 medium yellow capsicum (200g), sliced thickly
1 medium green capsicum (200g), sliced thickly

1 Heat half the oil in large saucepan; cook chicken, in batches, until browned all over.
2 Heat remaining oil in pan; cook onion, garlic, chilli and cumin, stirring, until onion softens.
3 Return chicken to pan with tomato, stock and ¼ cup of the oregano; bring to the boil. Reduce heat; simmer, covered, 30 minutes. Add beans and capsicums; simmer, uncovered, 20 minutes.
4 Divide stew among bowls; sprinkle with remaining oregano. Serve with sour cream, if desired.

preparation time 20 minutes **cooking time** 1 hour
serves 4
nutritional count per serving 26.5g total fat (7.1g saturated fat); 2090kJ (500 cal); 19.0g carbohydrate; 42.6g protein; 8.4g fibre

Chicken and broad bean fricassee

4 chicken breast fillets (800g), halved
¼ cup (40g) plain flour
½ teaspoon salt
½ teaspoon cracked black pepper
2 teaspoons olive oil
20g butter
400g baby chat potatoes, sliced thinly
400g baby carrots
2 cups (500ml) chicken stock
2 cups (300g) frozen broad beans, peeled
¼ cup (60ml) sour cream
2 teaspoons tarragon leaves

1 Toss the chicken in combined flour, salt and pepper; shake away excess flour.
2 Heat oil and butter in a large, deep frying pan; cook chicken until well browned all over and almost cooked through. Remove from pan.
3 Add potatoes and carrots to same pan; cook, stirring, 1 minute. Stir in stock; bring to the boil. Simmer, covered, about 5 minutes or until vegetables are almost tender.
4 Return chicken to pan, simmer, covered, for about 5 minutes or until heated through. Add beans and sour cream; stir until heated through.
5 Serve topped with tarragon.

preparation time 25 minutes **cooking time** 35 minutes
serves 4
nutritional count per serving 18.1g total fat (8.5g saturated fat); 2119kJ (507 cal); 27.3g carbohydrate; 54.6g protein; 8.0g fibre

Anise and ginger braised duck

1.7kg duck
¼ cup (60ml) sweet sherry
1 cup (250ml) water
2 tablespoons soy sauce
4 cloves garlic, sliced thinly
3cm piece fresh ginger (15g), sliced thinly
3 star anise
1 teaspoon sambal oelek
1 teaspoon cornflour
2 teaspoons water, extra

1 Using knife or poultry shears, cut down either side of duck backbone; discard backbone. Cut duck in half through breastbone, then cut each half into two pieces. Trim excess fat from duck, leaving skin intact.
2 Place duck pieces in single layer, skin-side down, in large saucepan; cook over low heat about 10 minutes or until skin is crisp. Drain on absorbent paper.
3 Place duck in clean saucepan with sherry, the water, sauce, garlic, ginger, star anise and sambal oelek; simmer, covered, about 1½ hours or until duck is very tender. Turn duck halfway through cooking. Cover undrained duck mixture; refrigerate overnight.
4 Next day, discard fat layer from surface; place duck mixture in large saucepan. Cook, covered, over low heat until duck is heated through. Remove duck from pan; keep warm.
5 Strain liquid into small saucepan; stir in blended cornflour and extra water. Stir over heat until mixture boils and thickens slightly.
6 Serve sauce over duck with steamed buk choy, if desired.

preparation time 30 minutes (plus refrigeration time)
cooking time 2 hours **serves** 4
nutritional count per serving 89.5g total fat (26.9g saturated fat); 3979kJ (952 cal); 3.3g carbohydrate; 32.3g protein; 0.7g fibre

Asian chicken pot au feu

4 litres (16 cups) water
1.5kg chicken
2 cloves garlic, bruised
2 large carrots (360g), halved, quartered lengthways
10cm stick fresh lemon grass (20g), bruised
2 fresh kaffir lime leaves
2cm piece galangal (10g), sliced thinly
2 fresh long red chillies, halved lengthways
1 teaspoon sichuan peppercorns
½ teaspoon five-spice powder
¼ cup (60ml) mirin
½ cup (125ml) soy sauce
⅓ cup (80ml) kecap manis
350g broccolini, chopped coarsely

1 Bring the water to the boil in large deep saucepan. Add chicken, garlic, carrot, lemon grass, lime leaves, galangal, chilli, peppercorns, five-spice, mirin, sauce and kecap manis; return to the boil. Reduce heat; simmer, uncovered, 1 hour, skimming fat from surface occasionally.
2 Remove chicken; strain broth through muslin-lined sieve into large bowl. Reserve carrot; discard remaining solids. Cover chicken and carrot to keep warm.
3 Return all but 2 cups of the broth to same saucepan; bring to the boil. Add broccolini; cook, uncovered, until just tender, drain over large bowl. Reserve broth for another use.
4 Meanwhile, place the reserved broth in small saucepan; bring to the boil. Boil rapidly, uncovered, until reduced to 1 cup.
5 Serve chicken with carrot, broccolini, reduced broth and, if desired, steamed jasmine rice.

preparation time 30 minutes **cooking time** 1 hour 30 minutes
serves 4
nutritional count per serving 28.6g total fat (8.8g saturated fat); 2082kJ (498 cal); 16.0g carbohydrate; 41.8g protein; 6.0g fibre

Chicken, olive and lemon tagine

1 cup (200g) dried chickpeas
8 chicken drumsticks (1.2kg)
8 chicken thigh cutlets (1.3kg)
2 tablespoons plain flour
2 teaspoons hot paprika
40g butter
2 medium red onions (340g), sliced thickly
3 cloves garlic, crushed
1 teaspoon cumin seeds
½ teaspoon ground turmeric
½ teaspoon ground coriander
¼ teaspoon saffron threads
1 teaspoon dried chilli flakes
1 teaspoon ground ginger
3 cups (750ml) chicken stock
2 tablespoons finely sliced preserved lemon rind
⅓ cup (40g) seeded green olives
2 tablespoons finely chopped fresh coriander

1 Place chickpeas in medium bowl, cover with water; stand overnight, drain. Rinse under cold water; drain. Place chickpeas in medium saucepan of boiling water; bring to the boil. Reduce heat; simmer, uncovered, about 40 minutes or until chickpeas are tender.
2 Preheat oven to 160°C/140°C fan-forced.
3 Coat chicken pieces in combined flour and paprika; shake away any excess flour mixture. Melt butter in large flameproof casserole dish; cook chicken pieces, in batches, until browned.
4 Cook onion in same dish, stirring, until softened. Add garlic, cumin, turmeric, ground coriander, saffron, chilli and ginger; cook, stirring, until fragrant. Return chicken with stock to dish; bring to the boil, then cook, covered, in oven 30 minutes. Add drained chickpeas; cook, covered, 1 hour.
5 Stir in lemon, olives and fresh coriander just before serving; serve with steamed rice, if desired.

preparation time 20 minutes (plus standing time)
cooking time 2 hours 45 minutes **serves** 8
nutritional count per serving 32.0g total fat (11.5g saturated fat);
2057kJ (492 cal); 10.4g carbohydrate; 39.8g protein; 2.6g fibre

One-pot spiced chicken, pumpkin and rice

2 tablespoons olive oil
750g butternut pumpkin, diced into 3cm pieces
500g chicken thigh fillets, chopped coarsely
1 large brown onion (200g), sliced thinly
1 teaspoon ground coriander
½ teaspoon ground cinnamon
½ teaspoon ground ginger
¼ teaspoon ground nutmeg
pinch saffron threads
2 cups (400g) basmati rice, washed, drained
3 cups (750ml) chicken stock
1 tablespoon currants
½ cup (80g) coarsely chopped almond kernels, roasted
¼ cup (35g) coarsely chopped dried apricots
¾ cup coarsely chopped fresh coriander
½ cup (140g) plain yogurt
1 tablespoon lime juice

1 Heat 1 tablespoon of the oil in large saucepan; cook pumpkin, over high heat, stirring occasionally, until browned. Remove from pan.
2 Heat remaining oil in the same pan; cook chicken, in batches, until browned all over. Remove from pan.
3 Cook onion in same pan, stirring, until soft. Add spices and saffron; stir until fragrant. Add rice; stir 1 minute, then stir in stock. Place chicken, pumpkin and currants on top of rice; bring to the boil. Reduce heat; simmer, covered tightly, for 10 minutes or until stock is absorbed and rice is tender. Add almonds, apricots and coriander, stir gently to combine.
4 Serve with combined yogurt and juice, and extra lime wedges, if desired.

preparation time 15 minutes **cooking time** 35 minutes
serves 6
nutritional count per serving 21.7g total fat (4.3g saturated fat); 2466kJ (590 cal); 68.1g carbohydrate; 28.2g protein; 4.3g fibre

seafood

Sri Lankan crab curry

1 tablespoon peanut oil
2 large brown onions (400g), chopped finely
4 cloves garlic, crushed
3cm piece fresh ginger (15g), grated
1 fresh small red thai chilli, chopped finely
4 dried curry leaves
½ teaspoon fenugreek seeds
1 teaspoon ground cinnamon
1 teaspoon ground turmeric
2 x 400ml cans coconut cream
1 tablespoon fish sauce
2 tablespoons lime juice
2 whole cooked mud crabs (1.6kg)
½ cup (25g) coconut flakes, toasted

1 Heat oil in wok; stir-fry onion, garlic, ginger and chilli until onion softens. Add curry leaves and spices; stir-fry until fragrant. Add coconut cream, sauce and juice; simmer, uncovered, 30 minutes.
2 Meanwhile, lift tail flap of each crab then, with a peeling motion, lift off the back of each shell. Remove and discard the gills, liver and brain matter; rinse crabs well. Cut each body in half; separate claws from bodies. You will have eight pieces.
3 Add half of the crab to wok; simmer, covered, about 10 minutes or until crab is heated through. Transfer crab to large serving bowl; cover to keep warm. Repeat with remaining crab pieces.
4 Spoon curry sauce over crab; sprinkle with coconut.

preparation time 30 minutes **cooking time** 55 minutes
serves 4
nutritional count per serving 52.5g total fat (37.2g saturated fat); 3118kJ (746 cal); 14.4g carbohydrate; 51.9g protein; 6.4g fibre

Red emperor in thai-style coconut sauce

1 ½ cups (300g) jasmine rice
3 ¼ cups (800ml) coconut milk
4 kaffir lime leaves, sliced thinly
2 fresh red thai chillies, sliced thinly
4cm piece fresh ginger (20g), chopped finely
1 tablespoon fish sauce
2 tablespoons lime juice
1 tablespoon finely chopped fresh coriander root
1 tablespoon finely chopped fresh lemon grass
1 tablespoon grated palm sugar
4 red emperor fillets (800g), skinned
⅓ cup firmly packed fresh coriander leaves

1 Cook rice in large saucepan of boiling water, uncovered, until just tender; drain.
2 Meanwhile, combine coconut milk, lime leaves, chilli, ginger, sauce, juice, coriander root, lemon grass and sugar in large frying pan; bring to the boil. Reduce heat; simmer, uncovered, 10 minutes. Add fish; simmer, covered, about 10 minutes or until fish is cooked through. Remove from heat; stir in coriander.
3 Serve fish with coconut sauce on rice.

preparation time 20 minutes **cooking time** 25 minutes
serves 4
nutritional count per serving 46.2g total fat (37.8g saturated fat); 3800kJ (909 cal); 70.7g carbohydrate; 50.3g protein; 4.4g fibre
tip Any other firm white fish fillet, such as ling or perch, can be used in this recipe; cooking times will vary, depending on the fish used.

Fish curry with coriander and snake beans

50g butter
1 small brown onion (80g), chopped finely
3 cloves garlic, crushed
4cm piece fresh ginger (20g), grated
1 fresh long red chilli, slice thinly
½ teaspoon ground turmeric
1½ teaspoons sweet paprika
2 teaspoons ground coriander
1 cup (250ml) coconut milk
½ cup (125ml) water
2 teaspoons tamarind puree
1 teaspoon salt
250g snake beans, cut into 5cm lengths
700g blue-eye fillets, chopped coarsely
½ cup loosely packed fresh coriander leaves

1 Heat the butter in large saucepan; cook onion, garlic and ginger, stirring, until soft. Add chilli; cook, stirring 1 minute. Add turmeric, paprika and coriander; cook, stirring over low heat, for 5 minutes or until fragrant.
2 Add the coconut milk, water, tamarind and salt; bring to the boil. Add the beans and fish, simmer, uncovered, for about 5 minutes or until fish is just cooked through.
3 Top curry with the coriander and serve with steamed basmati rice and naan bread, if desired.

preparation time 15 minutes **cooking time** 15 minutes
serves 4
nutritional count per serving 27.3g total fat (19.3g saturated fat); 1806kJ (432 cal); 5.4g carbohydrate; 39.7g protein; 3.8g fibre

Mussels with beer

1kg large black mussels
1 tablespoon olive oil
2 cloves garlic, crushed
1 large red onion (300g), sliced thinly
2 fresh long red chillies, sliced thinly
1 ½ cups (375ml) beer
2 tablespoons sweet chilli sauce
1 cup coarsely chopped fresh flat-leaf parsley
garlic bread
1 loaf turkish bread (430g)
50g butter, melted
2 cloves garlic, crushed
2 tablespoons finely chopped fresh flat-leaf parsley

1 Scrub mussels; remove beards.
2 Make garlic bread.
3 Meanwhile, heat oil on heated barbecue flat plate; cook garlic, onion and chilli, stirring, until onion softens. Add mussels and combined beer and chilli sauce; cook, covered, about 5 minutes or until mussels open (discard any that do not). Remove from heat; stir in parsley.
4 Serve mussels with garlic bread.
garlic bread Halve bread horizontally; cut each half into four pieces, brush with combined butter, garlic and parsley. Cook bread on heated oiled grill plate, uncovered, until browned both sides.

preparation time 20 minutes **cooking time** 15 minutes
serves 4
nutritional count per serving 19.7g total fat (8.3g saturated fat); 2174kJ (520 cal); 58.3g carbohydrate; 17.6g protein; 5.6g fibre

Kingfish and tomato tagine

2 tablespoons olive oil
2 large brown onions (400g), chopped coarsely
6 cloves garlic, chopped finely
1 fresh small red thai chilli, chopped finely
4 drained anchovy fillets, chopped finely
¾ cup coarsely chopped fresh flat-leaf parsley
1 cup coarsely chopped fresh coriander
¾ cup coarsely chopped fresh mint
200g mushrooms, quartered
2 trimmed celery stalks (200g), sliced thickly
2 teaspoons ground cumin
2 x 425g cans diced tomatoes
4 kingfish cutlets (1kg)
1 medium lemon (140g), cut into wedges
2 tablespoons fresh flat-leaf parsley leaves

1 Preheat oven to 200°C/180°C fan-forced.
2 Heat oil in large deep flameproof baking dish; cook onion, garlic and chilli, stirring, until onion softens. Add anchovy, chopped herbs, mushrooms, celery and cumin; cook, stirring, 5 minutes.
3 Add undrained tomatoes; bring to the boil. Add fish, submerging it in the tomato mixture; return to the boil. Cook, uncovered, in oven about 20 minutes or until liquid has almost evaporated and fish is cooked as desired.
4 Divide fish and lemon wedge among serving plates; sprinkle with parsley. Serve with a tomato and herb salad and steamed rice, if desired.

preparation time 20 minutes **cooking time** 40 minutes
serves 4
nutritional count per serving 14.9g total fat (3.0g saturated fat); 1655kJ (396 cal); 13.6g carbohydrate; 47.9g protein; 7.9g fibre

Malaysian fish curry

2 tablespoons vegetable oil
1⅔ cups (400ml) coconut milk
1 cup (250ml) coconut cream
2 cups (400g) jasmine rice
4 blue-eye fillets (800g), skinless
⅓ cup (15g) flaked coconut, toasted
4 fresh kaffir lime leaves, sliced thinly
spice paste
4 shallots (100g), quartered
10cm piece fresh galangal (50g), quartered
½ teaspoon ground turmeric
½ teaspoon fennel seeds
1 teaspoon ground coriander
¼ cup (75g) madras curry paste
2 tablespoons lime juice
2 cloves garlic, quartered
4 fresh small red thai chillies
1 teaspoon caster sugar

1 Blend or process ingredients for spice paste until smooth.
2 Heat half of the oil in large frying pan; cook paste, stirring, over medium heat until fragrant. Add coconut milk and cream; bring to the boil. Reduce heat; simmer, uncovered, about 15 minutes or until curry sauce thickens slightly.
3 Meanwhile, cook rice in large saucepan of boiling water, uncovered, until tender; drain. Cover to keep warm.
4 Heat remaining oil in large frying pan; cook fish, uncovered, about 10 minutes or until cooked as desired.
5 Divide fish among shallow serving bowls; top with curry sauce, sprinkle with coconut and lime leaves. Serve rice in separate bowl; sprinkle curry with sliced chilli, if desired.

preparation time 15 minutes **cooking time** 30 minutes
serves 4
nutritional count per serving 56.2g total fat (34.9g saturated fat); 4468kJ (1069 cal); 89.0g carbohydrate; 52.4g protein; 6.7g fibre

Lemon, coconut and chilli poached fish

You can use any firm white fish fillet, such as ling, perch or blue eye, in this recipe.

1½ cups (300g) jasmine rice
400ml can coconut cream
2 tablespoons fish sauce
1 tablespoon finely grated lemon rind
¼ cup (60ml) lemon juice
2 fresh long red chillies, chopped finely
3cm piece fresh ginger (15g), grated
4 x 200g firm white fish fillets
¼ cup fresh coriander leaves

1 Cook rice in large saucepan of boiling water, uncovered, until just tender; drain.
2 Meanwhile, combine coconut cream, sauce, rind, juice, chilli and ginger in medium frying pan; bring to the boil. Reduce heat; simmer, uncovered, 10 minutes. Add fish; simmer, covered, about 10 minutes or until cooked as desired. Remove from heat; stir in coriander.
3 Divide rice among serving dishes; top with fish and drizzle with coconut cream sauce.

preparation time 15 minutes **cooking time** 25 minutes
serves 4
nutritional count per serving 26.8g total fat (20.4g saturated fat); 2955kJ (707 cal); 64.4g carbohydrate; 49.6g protein; 4.0g fibre

Octopus braised in red wine

⅓ cup (80ml) olive oil
600g baby onions, halved
4 cloves garlic, crushed
1.5kg cleaned baby octopus, halved
1½ cups (375ml) dry red wine
⅓ cup (95g) tomato paste
⅓ cup (80ml) red wine vinegar
3 large tomatoes (660g), peeled, seeded, chopped coarsely
2 bay leaves
1 fresh long red chilli, chopped finely
10 drained anchovy fillets (30g), chopped coarsely
⅓ cup finely chopped fresh oregano
1 cup coarsely chopped fresh flat-leaf parsley

1 Heat oil in large saucepan; cook onion and garlic, stirring, until onion softens. Add octopus; cook, stirring, until just changed in colour.
2 Add wine; cook, stirring, about 5 minutes or until pan liquid is reduced by about a third. Add paste, vinegar, fresh tomato, bay leaves, chilli and anchovies; bring to the boil. Reduce heat; simmer, covered, 1 hour. Remove lid; simmer about 30 minutes or until sauce thickens and octopus is tender. Remove and discard bay leaves.
3 Stir in oregano and parsley off the heat; serve with thick slices of toasted Italian ciabatta, if desired.

preparation time 15 minutes **cooking time** 1 hour 45 minutes
serves 6
nutritional count per serving 14.7g total fat (1.8g saturated fat); 1597kJ (382 cal); 5.6g carbohydrate; 45.0g protein; 2.8g fibre

Japanese seafood hotpot

We used monkfish in this recipe, but you can use any firm white fish such as perch or blue-eye fillets.

12 medium black mussels (300g)
12 uncooked medium king prawns (540g)
2 teaspoons cooking sake
1 tablespoon japanese soy sauce
2 teaspoons mirin
12 scallops without roe (300g)
400g firm white fish fillets, diced into 4cm pieces
1 tablespoon vegetable oil
2 cloves garlic, crushed
5cm piece fresh ginger (25g), chopped finely
3 cups (750ml) fish stock
1 cup (250ml) water
¼ cup (60ml) cooking sake, extra
¼ cup (60ml) japanese soy sauce, extra
1 teaspoon dashi powder
1 small kumara (250g), halved lengthways, sliced thinly
250g spinach, chopped coarsely
2 green onions, chopped coarsely
270g dried udon noodles

1 Scrub mussels; remove beards. Shell and devein prawns, leaving tails intact. Combine sake, soy and mirin in large bowl; add mussels, prawns, scallops and fish, toss seafood to coat in mixture.
2 Heat oil in large saucepan; cook garlic and ginger, stirring, until fragrant. Add stock, the water, extra sake, extra soy and dashi; bring to the boil. Add kumara; cook, uncovered, 2 minutes. Add undrained seafood; cook, covered, about 5 minutes or until mussels open (discard any that do not). Add spinach and onion; cook, uncovered, until spinach just wilts.
3 Meanwhile, cook noodles in large saucepan of boiling water, uncovered, until just tender; drain.
4 Divide noodles among bowls; top with seafood mixture.

preparation time 20 minutes (plus refrigeration time)
cooking time 20 minutes **serves** 4
nutritional count per serving 7.8g total fat (1.3g saturated fat);
2307kJ (552 cal); 57.3g carbohydrate; 56.8g protein; 4.5g fibre

Quick lemon grass and coconut fish stew

250g dried egg noodles
8 dried shiitake mushrooms
1 tablespoon vegetable oil
2 teaspoons grated fresh ginger
10cm stick fresh lemon grass (20g), chopped finely
½ teaspoon five-spice powder
1 teaspoon ground turmeric
1 teaspoon sambal oelek
400ml can coconut cream
¼ cup (60ml) chicken stock
1kg boneless white fish fillets, chopped coarsely
400g baby buk choy, quartered
4 green onions, chopped finely

1 Cook noodles in large saucepan of boiling water, uncovered, until just tender; drain.
2 Place mushrooms in large heatproof bowl; cover with boiling water. Stand 20 minutes; drain mushrooms. Discard stems; slice caps.
3 Heat oil in large saucepan; cook ginger, lemon grass, spices, sambal oelek and mushrooms, stirring, until fragrant. Add coconut cream and stock; bring to the boil. Add fish; reduce heat. Cook, covered, 10 minutes or until fish is just tender.
4 Stir in buk choy, onion and noodles; reheat gently.

preparation time 20 minutes (plus standing time)
cooking time 30 minutes **serves** 6
nutritional count per serving 21.4g total fat (13.8g saturated fat); 2094kJ (501 cal); 33.1g carbohydrate; 42.0g protein; 3.6g fibre

Anchovy and garlic tuna with tomato and oregano

1kg tuna fillet, trimmed, skinned
3 cloves garlic, sliced thinly
¼ cup firmly packed fresh oregano leaves
8 drained anchovy fillets, halved
¼ cup (60ml) olive oil
1 large brown onion (200g), sliced thinly
4 large egg tomatoes (360g), seeded, chopped coarsely
¼ cup (60ml) balsamic vinegar
2 tablespoons dry white wine
¼ cup (60ml) fish stock
1 tablespoon drained baby capers, rinsed
¼ cup coarsely chopped fresh basil

1 Preheat oven to 200°C/180°C fan-forced.
2 Using sharp knife, make 16 cuts in tuna; press 16 slices of the garlic, 16 oregano leaves and anchovy halves into cuts.
3 Heat 2 tablespoons of the oil in medium deep flameproof baking dish; cook tuna, uncovered, until browned. Remove from dish.
4 Heat remaining oil in same dish; cook onion, stirring, until soft. Combine tomato, vinegar, wine, stock, remaining garlic and remaining oregano in dish then add tuna; bring to the boil. Cook, uncovered, in oven about 10 minutes or until tuna is cooked as desired. Remove tuna from dish; slice thinly. Stir capers and basil into sauce in dish.
5 Serve tuna with sauce and, if desired, mashed potato (see page 360).

preparation time 20 minutes **cooking time** 25 minutes
serves 4
nutritional count per serving 28.7g total fat (7.8g saturated fat); 2286kJ (547 cal); 4.1g carbohydrate; 65.8g protein; 1.6g fibre

Assamese sour fish curry

1 tablespoon coriander seeds
2 teaspoons cumin seeds
½ teaspoon ground turmeric
1 teaspoon black peppercorns
2cm piece fresh ginger (10g), chopped coarsely
2 cloves garlic, chopped coarsely
2 long green chillies, chopped coarsely
2 tablespoons vegetable oil
4 blue-eye cutlets (800g)
2 medium brown onions (300g), sliced thinly
1½ teaspoons black mustard seeds
4 fresh curry leaves
¾ cup (180ml) water
⅓ cup (80ml) fish stock
¼ cup (60ml) lime juice
1 tablespoon fish sauce

1 Dry-fry coriander and cumin seeds and turmeric in small frying pan, stirring, until fragrant. Using mortar and pestle, crush spices with peppercorns, ginger, garlic and chilli to form a paste.
2 Heat half of the oil in large frying pan; cook fish, uncovered, until browned both sides. Remove from pan; cover to keep warm.
3 Heat remaining oil in same pan; cook onion, mustard seeds and curry leaves, stirring, about 5 minutes or until onion is browned lightly. Add spice paste; cook, stirring, until fragrant. Add the water, stock, juice and sauce; bring to the boil. Return fish to pan; simmer, covered, about 5 minutes or until fish is cooked as desired.

preparation time 20 minutes **cooking time** 20 minutes
serves 4
nutritional count per serving 12.9g total fat (2.3g saturated fat); 1150kJ (275 cal); 3.8g carbohydrate; 34.7g protein; 1.6g fibre

Prawn fricassee with sumac, leek and peas

24 uncooked medium king prawns (1kg)
¼ cup (60ml) olive oil
2 tablespoons sumac
10g butter
1 medium leek (350g), sliced thinly
1 clove garlic, crushed
½ cup (125ml) dry white wine
2 cups (500ml) chicken stock
2 teaspoons wholegrain mustard
⅓ cup (80ml) cream
1 cup (120g) frozen peas
2 large egg tomatoes (180g), chopped finely
2 tablespoons coarsely chopped fresh tarragon

1 Shell and devein prawns, leaving tails intact. Combine 1 tablespoon of the oil with sumac in medium bowl, add prawns; toss prawns to coat in mixture. Cover; refrigerate 30 minutes.
2 Heat butter and another 1 tablespoon of the oil in large deep frying pan; cook prawns, stirring, until just changed in colour. Transfer to medium bowl.
3 Heat remaining oil in same pan; cook leek and garlic, stirring, until leek is almost tender. Add wine; cook, uncovered, until wine is almost evaporated. Add stock; bring to the boil. Reduce heat; simmer, uncovered, about 10 minutes or until liquid is reduced by a third.
4 Add mustard and cream; bring to the boil. Return prawns to pan with peas; stir until prawns are just cooked and peas are tender.
5 Remove from heat; stir in tomato and tarragon. Serve with steamed jasmine rice, if desired.

preparation time 25 minutes (plus refrigeration time)
cooking time 30 minutes **serves** 4
nutritional count per serving 24.8g total fat; 8.5g saturated fat; 1668kJ (399 cal); 6.2g carbohydrate; 33.2g protein; 3.8g fibre

Cioppino

2 teaspoons olive oil
1 medium brown onion (150g), chopped coarsely
1 baby fennel bulb (130g), trimmed, chopped coarsely
3 cloves garlic, crushed
6 medium tomatoes (1kg), chopped coarsely
425g can crushed tomatoes
½ cup (125ml) dry white wine
1½ cups (375ml) fish stock
2 cooked blue swimmer crabs (700g)
500g uncooked large king prawns
450g swordfish steaks
400g clams, rinsed
150g scallops
¼ cup coarsely chopped fresh basil
½ cup coarsely chopped fresh flat-leaf parsley

1 Heat oil in large saucepan; cook onion, fennel and garlic, stirring, until onion softens. Add fresh tomato; cook, stirring, about 5 minutes or until pulpy. Stir in undrained crushed tomatoes, wine and stock; reduce heat, simmer, covered, 20 minutes.
2 Meanwhile, remove back shell from crabs; discard grey gills. Rinse crab; using sharp knife, chop each crab into four pieces. Shell and devein prawns, leaving tails intact. Chop fish into 2cm pieces.
3 Add clams to pan; simmer, covered, about 5 minutes or until clams open (discard any that do not). Add remaining seafood; cook, stirring occasionally, about 5 minutes or until seafood has changed in colour and is cooked as desired. Remove from heat; stir in herbs.

preparation time 30 minutes **cooking time** 40 minutes
serves 4
nutritional count per serving 6.4g total fat (1.4g saturated fat); 1476kJ (352 cal); 13.1g carbohydrate; 54.2g protein; 5.9g fibre

Coconut fish curry

We used ling in this recipe, but you can use any firm white fish fillet such as perch or blue-eye fillets.

¼ cup (60ml) vegetable oil
800g firm white fish fillets, diced into 3cm pieces
1 medium brown onion (150g), sliced thinly
2 cloves garlic, crushed
2 long green chillies, sliced thinly
3 teaspoons garam masala
1⅔ cups (410ml) coconut milk
2 tablespoons lemon juice
¼ cup (60ml) tamarind concentrate
1 large tomato (220g), chopped coarsely
1 medium red capsicum (200g), chopped coarsely
⅓ cup firmly packed fresh coriander leaves
1 medium lemon (140g), cut into wedges

1 Heat 2 tablespoons of the oil in large saucepan; cook fish, in batches, until browned all over.
2 Heat remaining oil in same pan; cook onion, garlic and half of the chilli, stirring, until onion softens. Add garam masala; cook, stirring, until fragrant. Add coconut milk, juice, tamarind, tomato and capsicum; bring to the boil. Add fish, reduce heat; simmer, covered, about 5 minutes or until fish is cooked as desired.
3 Divide curry among serving bowls; top with coriander and remaining chilli. Serve with lemon wedges and your choice of warmed Indian naan, chapati or pappadum, if desired.

preparation time 25 minutes **cooking time** 20 minutes
serves 4
nutritional count per serving 36.5g total fat (20.6g saturated fat); 2257kJ (540 cal); 9.1g carbohydrate; 43.7g protein; 4.6g fibre

Baby octopus and eggplant in tomato and caper sauce

1 tablespoon olive oil
1.2kg whole cleaned baby octopus
1 clove garlic, sliced thinly
3 shallots (75g), sliced thinly
4 baby eggplants (240g), sliced thinly
1 medium red capsicum (200g), sliced thinly
½ cup (125ml) dry red wine
700g bottled tomato pasta sauce
⅓ cup (80ml) water
¼ cup (40g) drained baby capers, rinsed
2 tablespoons coarsely chopped fresh oregano

1 Heat half of the oil in large deep frying pan; cook octopus, in batches, until just changed in colour and tender. Cover to keep warm.
2 Heat remaining oil in same pan; cook garlic and shallot, stirring, until shallot softens. Add eggplant and capsicum; cook, stirring, 5 minutes or until vegetables are just tender.
3 Add wine to pan with sauce, the water and octopus; bring to the boil. Reduce heat; simmer, covered, about 10 minutes or until sauce thickens slightly. Stir in capers and oregano.
4 Top with extra oregano leaves and serve with steamed rice, if desired.

preparation time 10 minutes **cooking time** 25 minutes
serves 4
nutritional count per serving 8.2g total fat (0.8g saturated fat); 1701kJ (407 cal); 21.4g carbohydrate; 53.4g protein; 5.4g fibre

Marinara with buckwheat noodles

500g vongole (clams)
2 tablespoons rock salt
16 uncooked medium king prawns (720g)
400g kingfish
400g cleaned squid hoods
1 tablespoon olive oil
1 medium red onion (170g), chopped finely
2 cloves garlic, crushed
1 medium red capsicum (200g), chopped coarsely
½ cup (125ml) white wine
800g can diced tomatoes
½ teaspoon dried chilli flakes
375g buckwheat noodles

1 Place vongole and salt in large bowl, cover with cold water. Refrigerate for 1 hour to purge any grit. Drain and rinse well.
2 Shell and devein prawns, leaving tails intact. Remove skin and bones from fish; chop flesh coarsely.
3 Heat oil in large saucepan; cook onion, garlic and capsicum, stirring, until onion softens. Add wine; bring to the boil. Reduce heat; simmer, uncovered, 5 minutes. Add tomatoes and chilli; simmer about 20 minutes.
4 Add seafood; cook, stirring occasionally, about 8 minutes or until cooked through.
5 Cook noodles in large saucepan of boiling water until just tender; drain.
6 Serve marinara with noodles.

preparation time 25 minutes (plus refrigeration time)
cooking time 35 minutes **serves** 4
nutritional count per serving 10.3g total fat (2.2g saturated fat); 3035kJ (726 cal); 74.7g carbohydrate; 73.6g protein; 6.8g fibre

Seafood stew with chermoulla

500g black mussels
800g uncooked medium king prawns
300g kingfish fillet, skinned
1 squid hood (150g)
1 tablespoon olive oil
1 large brown onion (200g), chopped finely
3 cloves garlic, crushed
1 medium red capsicum (200g), chopped finely
½ cup (125ml) dry white wine
1 cup (250ml) fish stock
400g can diced tomatoes
chermoulla
½ cup finely chopped fresh coriander
½ cup finely chopped fresh flat-leaf parsley
1 clove garlic, crushed
2 tablespoons white wine vinegar
2 tablespoons lemon juice
½ teaspoon ground cumin
2 tablespoons olive oil

1 Scrub mussels; remove beards. Shell and devein prawns, leaving tails intact. Dice fish into 3cm pieces. Cut squid down centre to open out; score inside in diagonal pattern then cut into thick strips.
2 Heat oil in large saucepan; cook onion, garlic and capsicum, stirring, until onion softens. Stir in wine; cook, uncovered, until wine is almost evaporated. Add stock and undrained tomatoes; bring to the boil. Add seafood, reduce heat; simmer, covered, about 5 minutes or until squid is tender and mussels open (discard any that do not).
3 Meanwhile, combine ingredients for chermoulla in small bowl.
4 Stir half of the chermoulla into stew. Divide stew among serving bowls; divide remaining chermoulla over the top of each bowl. Serve with a warmed baguette, if desired.

preparation time 30 minutes **cooking time** 30 minutes
serves 4
nutritional count per serving 17.5g total fat (3g saturated fat); 1714kJ (410 cal); 8.7g carbohydrate; 48.6g protein; 3.5g fibre

Stuffed squid saganaki

8 small whole squid (600g)
¼ cup (40g) seeded kalamata olives, chopped coarsely
1 teaspoon finely grated lemon rind
¼ teaspoon dried chilli flakes
200g fetta cheese, crumbled
2 teaspoons fresh thyme leaves
1 tablespoon olive oil
1 small red onion (100g), chopped finely
1 clove garlic, crushed
½ cup (125ml) dry white wine
1 cinnamon stick
2 x 400g cans diced tomatoes
3 sprigs fresh thyme
2 teaspoons white sugar

1 Gently separate bodies and tentacles of squid by pulling on tentacles.
Cut head from tentacles just below eyes; discard head. Trim long tentacle
of each squid; remove the clear quill from inside body. Peel inside flaps
from bodies with salted fingers, then peel away dark skin. Wash squid
well and pat dry with absorbent paper.
2 Combine olives, rind, chilli, three-quarters of the cheese and half of
the thyme leaves in small bowl; stuff cheese mixture into squid bodies.
Place tentacles inside opening; secure tentacles to squid with toothpicks.
Cover; refrigerate until required.
3 Heat oil in large deep frying pan; cook onion and garlic, stirring,
until onion softens. Add wine; bring to the boil. Reduce heat; simmer,
uncovered, until liquid is reduced by half.
4 Add cinnamon, undrained tomatoes, thyme sprigs and sugar; bring
to the boil. Reduce heat; simmer, uncovered, 10 minutes or until sauce
thickens slightly. Add stuffed squid to pan; simmer, covered, 15 minutes
or until squid are cooked through, turning once halfway through cooking
time. Add remaining cheese and remaining thyme leaves; stir until cheese
melts slightly. Remove toothpicks; serve with bread, if desired.

preparation time 50 minutes **cooking time** 45 minutes
serves 4
nutritional count per serving 18.6g total fat (8.9g saturated fat);
1580kJ (378 cal); 11.7g carbohydrate; 36.1g protein; 3.0g fibre

beef+veal

Veal shin on mushroom ragu

40g butter
4 pieces veal osso buco (1kg)
2 cloves garlic, crushed
1 tablespoon fresh rosemary leaves
½ cup (125ml) port
1 cup (250ml) beef stock
mushroom ragu
40g butter
2 cloves garlic, crushed
1 large flat mushroom (100g), sliced thickly
200g swiss brown mushrooms, trimmed
200g shiitake mushrooms, sliced thickly
1 medium red capsicum (200g), sliced thickly
1 medium green capsicum (200g), sliced thickly
½ cup (125ml) beef stock
2 tablespoons port

1 Preheat oven to 160°C/140°C fan-forced.
2 Melt butter in medium flameproof casserole dish; cook veal, uncovered, until browned both sides. Add garlic, rosemary, port and stock; cook, covered, in oven 2¼ hours.
3 Meanwhile, make mushroom ragu.
4 Divide veal and ragu among serving dishes; serve with soft polenta (see page 340), if desired.
mushroom ragu Heat butter in large frying pan; cook garlic, mushrooms and capsicums, stirring, until vegetables are browned lightly and tender. Stir in stock and port; cook, covered, 30 minutes.

preparation time 15 minutes **cooking time** 2 hours 15 minutes
serves 4
nutritional count per serving 17.9g total fat (11.1g saturated fat); 1743kJ (417 cal); 9.4g carbohydrate; 42.3g protein; 4.5g fibre

Beef and onion casserole

1kg beef chuck steak, diced into 2cm pieces
⅓ cup (50g) plain flour
2 tablespoons olive oil
2 small brown onions (200g), chopped coarsely
2 cloves garlic, crushed
150g mushrooms, quartered
1 cup (250ml) dry red wine
400g can crushed tomatoes
2 cups (500ml) beef stock
2 tablespoons tomato paste

1 Coat beef in flour, shake away excess. Heat half the oil in large saucepan; cook beef, in batches, until browned all over.
2 Heat remaining oil in same pan; cook onion, garlic and mushrooms, stirring, until onion softens.
3 Return beef to pan with wine, undrained tomatoes, stock and paste; bring to the boil. Reduce heat; simmer, covered, 40 minutes. Remove lid; simmer, stirring occasionally, about 40 minutes or until meat is tender and sauce thickens slightly.

preparation time 20 minutes **cooking time** 1 hour 30 minutes
serves 4
nutritional count per serving 21.2g total fat (6.2g saturated fat); 2245kJ (537 cal); 17.4g carbohydrate; 56.8g protein; 4.0g fibre

Family beef casserole

2 tablespoons vegetable oil
2kg beef chuck steak, chopped coarsely
2 medium brown onions (300g), sliced thinly
2 medium carrots (240g), sliced thickly
3 cloves garlic, crushed
¼ cup finely chopped fresh flat-leaf parsley
¼ cup (70g) tomato paste
2 teaspoons dijon mustard
1 cup (250ml) dry red wine
½ cup (125ml) beef stock

1 Preheat oven to 150°C/130°C fan-forced.
2 Heat oil in 2.5 litre (10-cup) flameproof casserole dish; cook beef, in batches, until browned.
3 Cook onion, carrot and garlic in same dish, stirring over heat, until onion is soft.
4 Return beef to dish; stir in parsley, paste, mustard, wine and stock. Cook, covered, in oven about 1¾ hours or until beef is tender.

preparation time 15 minutes **cooking time** 2 hours 15 minutes
serves 6
nutritional count per serving 21.4g total fat (7.1g saturated fat); 2203kJ (527 cal); 6.1g carbohydrate; 69.2g protein; 2.6g fibre

Borscht with meatballs

1 tablespoon olive oil
1 small brown onion (80g), chopped coarsely
1 small carrot (70g), chopped coarsely
1 small leek (200g), chopped coarsely
250g cabbage, chopped coarsely
1 large tomato (250g), chopped coarsely
2 medium beetroots (350g), peeled, chopped coarsely
2 veal shanks (1.5kg), trimmed, cut into thirds
1.25 litres (5 cups) water
500g beef mince
½ cup (100g) medium-grain white rice
1 teaspoon sweet paprika
1 small brown onion (80g), chopped finely
3 cloves garlic, crushed
½ cup finely chopped fresh flat-leaf parsley
2 eggs, beaten lightly
½ cup (120g) sour cream
2 tablespoons finely chopped fresh dill

1 Heat oil in large saucepan; cook coarsely chopped onion, carrot, leek, cabbage, tomato and beetroot, stirring, 15 minutes. Add veal and the water; bring to the boil. Reduce heat; simmer, covered, 1½ hours. Remove veal from pan; remove meat from shank and reserve for another use, if desired.
2 Meanwhile, using hands, combine mince, rice, paprika, finely chopped onion, garlic, parsley and egg in large bowl; shape rounded teaspoons of mince mixture into meatballs.
3 Return borscht to the boil; add meatballs. Reduce heat; simmer, uncovered, until meatballs are cooked through.
4 Divide borscht and meatballs among serving bowls; dollop with combined sour cream and dill. Serve with sliced rye or pumpernickel bread, if desired.

preparation time 20 minutes **cooking time** 2 hours
serves 4
nutritional count per serving 27.9g total fat (12.7g saturated fat);
3122kJ (747 cal); 34.4g carbohydrate; 84.9g protein; 8.2g fibre

Shredded Spanish beef

5 cloves garlic, quartered
1 large carrot (180g), chopped coarsely
1 trimmed celery stalk (100g), chopped coarsely
1.5kg beef skirt steak
6 black peppercorns
2 teaspoons dried oregano
2 litres (8 cups) water
2 tablespoons olive oil
2 rindless bacon rashers (130g), chopped finely
3 cloves garlic, extra, crushed
1 small brown onion (80g), chopped finely
½ small green capsicum (75g), chopped finely
1 tablespoon tomato paste
2 tablespoons red wine vinegar
1 medium red capsicum (200g), sliced thickly
1 medium green capsicum (200g), sliced thickly
2 medium brown onions (300g), sliced thickly
400g can whole tomatoes
1 teaspoon ground cumin
1 cup (150g) pimiento-stuffed green olives, halved
¼ cup (60ml) lemon juice

1 Place quartered garlic, carrot, celery, beef, peppercorns, half the oregano and the water in large deep saucepan; bring to the boil. Reduce heat; simmer, uncovered, 2 hours or until beef is tender.
2 Meanwhile, heat half of the oil in small frying pan; cook bacon, crushed garlic, finely chopped onion and finely chopped capsicum, stirring, until onion softens. Stir in paste and vinegar; cook until vinegar evaporates. Cool 10 minutes; blend or process until smooth.
3 Remove beef from braising liquid. Strain liquid over large bowl; discard solids. Using two forks, shred beef coarsely.
4 Heat remaining oil in same cleaned pan; cook capsicum mixture with thickly sliced capsicums and thickly sliced onion, stirring, until vegetables soften. Return beef and braising liquid to pan with undrained tomatoes, cumin and remaining oregano; bring to the boil. Reduce heat; simmer, uncovered, 20 minutes. Remove from heat; stir in olives and juice.
preparation time 40 minutes **cooking time** 2 hours 50 minutes
serves 6
nutritional count per serving 17.5g total fat (4.7g saturated fat); 1969kJ (471 cal); 11.0g carbohydrate; 64.0g protein; 6.2g fibre

Beef ragu with grilled polenta

1 litre (4 cups) water
1 teaspoon salt
1 cup (170g) polenta
½ cup (40g) finely grated parmesan cheese
1 egg yolk
1kg beef chuck steak, trimmed
2 tablespoons plain flour
1 tablespoon olive oil
20g butter
1 large brown onion (200g), chopped coarsely
2 cloves garlic, crushed
2 rindless bacon rashers (130g), chopped coarsely
200g button mushrooms, stems trimmed, halved
1 cup (250ml) dry red wine
1 cup (250ml) beef stock
¼ cup (70g) tomato paste
1 tablespoon dijon mustard
1 tablespoon finely chopped fresh thyme

1 Place the water and salt in large saucepan; bring to the boil. Gradually add polenta, stirring constantly. Reduce heat; simmer, uncovered, stirring constantly, about 20 minutes or until polenta thickens. Stir in cheese and egg yolk. Spread mixture evenly into oiled deep 19cm-square cake pan, pressing firmly. When cool, cover; refrigerate about 2 hours or until firm.
2 Meanwhile, cut beef into 3cm pieces, toss in flour; shake off excess.
3 Heat oil in large saucepan; cook beef, in batches, until browned all over.
4 Heat butter in same pan; cook onion, garlic, bacon and mushrooms, stirring, until onion softens. Return beef with any juices to pan. Add wine, stock, paste, mustard and thyme; bring to the boil. Reduce heat; simmer, covered, about 1¼ hours or until beef is tender, stirring occasionally.
5 Turn polenta onto board; trim edges. Cut polenta into four squares; cut each square in half diagonally. Cook polenta triangles on heated oiled grill plate (or grill or barbecue) until browned both sides.
6 Serve ragu over polenta triangles.

preparation time 20 minutes (plus refrigeration time)
cooking time 1 hour 30 minutes **serves** 4
nutritional count per serving 30.3g total fat (12.4g saturated fat); 3168kJ (758 cal); 38.9g carbohydrate; 69.6g protein; 4.4g fibre

Osso buco with artichoke and lemon

8 pieces veal osso buco (2kg)
¼ cup (35g) plain flour
1 tablespoon olive oil
30g butter
1 medium brown onion (150g), chopped finely
3 cloves garlic, sliced thinly
¾ cup (180ml) dry white wine
1 cup (250ml) beef stock
½ cup (125ml) water
400g bottled artichoke hearts, drained, halved
¼ cup (60ml) lemon juice
¼ cup coarsely chopped fresh flat-leaf parsley

1 Coat veal in flour; shake away excess. Heat half of the oil and half of the butter in large frying pan; cook veal, in batches, until browned all over. Stand veal upright in large deep ovenproof dish.
2 Preheat oven to 180°C/160°C fan-forced.
3 Heat remaining oil and butter in same pan; cook onion and garlic, stirring, until onion softens. Add wine, stock and the water; bring to the boil. Reduce heat; simmer, uncovered, about 5 minutes or until mixture reduces by a third.
4 Pour reduced mixture over veal in dish, cover with tight lid or foil; cook, covered, in oven 1¼ hours. Stir in artichoke; cook, covered, in oven a further 30 minutes or until veal is tender.
5 Serve veal and artichoke drizzled with juice and sprinkled with parsley.

preparation time 25 minutes **cooking time** 2 hours
serves 4
nutritional count per serving 12.6g total fat (5.1g saturated fat); 2036kJ (487 cal); 10.4g carbohydrate; 73.5g protein; 3.3g fibre

Braised beef cheeks in red wine

2 tablespoons olive oil
1.6kg beef cheeks, trimmed
1 medium brown onion (150g), chopped coarsely
1 medium carrot (120g), chopped coarsely
3 cups (750ml) dry red wine
¼ cup (60ml) red wine vinegar
2 x 400g cans whole tomatoes
¼ cup (55g) firmly packed brown sugar
6 black peppercorns
2 sprigs fresh rosemary
2 tablespoons fresh oregano leaves
1 large fennel bulb (550g), cut into thin wedges
400g spring onions, trimmed, halved
200g swiss brown mushrooms

1 Preheat oven to 160°C/140°C fan-forced.
2 Heat half of the oil in large flameproof casserole dish; cook beef, in batches, until browned all over.
3 Heat remaining oil in same dish; cook brown onion and carrot, stirring, until onion softens. Return beef to dish with wine, vinegar, undrained tomatoes, sugar, peppercorns, herbs and fennel; bring to the boil. Cook, covered, in oven for 2 hours.
4 Stir in spring onion and mushrooms; cook, uncovered, in oven a further 45 minutes or until beef is tender.
5 Serve beef with cheesy polenta (see page 367), if desired.

preparation time 20 minutes **cooking time** 3 hours 10 minutes
serves 4
nutritional count per serving 41.5g total fat (14.9g saturated fat); 4147kJ (992 cal); 29.2g carbohydrate; 89.9g protein; 8.9g fibre

Balti biryani

750g beef skirt steak, diced into 2cm pieces
¾ cup (225g) balti curry paste
2 cups (400g) basmati rice
8 cloves garlic, unpeeled
20g ghee
4 cardamom pods, bruised
4 cloves
1 cinnamon stick
3 green onions, sliced thinly
2 cups (500ml) beef stock
¾ cup (100g) roasted slivered almonds
¼ cup loosely packed fresh coriander leaves
2 fresh red thai chillies, sliced thinly

1 Preheat oven to 180°C/160°C fan-forced.
2 Combine steak and paste in medium bowl. Cover; refrigerate 1 hour.
3 Meanwhile, soak rice in medium bowl of cold water; stand 30 minutes. Drain rice in strainer; rinse under cold water, drain.
4 Meanwhile, place garlic in small baking dish; roast, uncovered, about 20 minutes or until softened.
5 Melt ghee in large saucepan; cook cardamom, cloves, cinnamon and onion, stirring, until fragrant. Add steak mixture, reduce heat; simmer, covered, stirring occasionally, about 45 minutes or until steak is tender.
6 Add rice to pan with stock; simmer, covered, stirring occasionally, about 15 minutes or until rice is just tender.
7 Peel garlic; chop finely. Add garlic, almonds and coriander to pan; cover then stand 5 minutes. Sprinkle biryani with chilli; serve with raita and naan, if desired.

preparation time 20 minutes (plus standing time)
cooking time 1 hour 30 minutes **serves** 4
nutritional count per serving 41.8g total fat (8.1g saturated fat); 4088kJ (978 cal); 86.2g carbohydrate; 58.9g protein; 10.0g fibre

Osso buco with tomatoes and olives

12 pieces veal osso buco (3kg)
¼ cup (35g) plain flour
¼ cup (60ml) olive oil
40g butter
1 medium brown onion (150g), chopped coarsely
2 cloves garlic, chopped finely
3 trimmed celery stalks (300g), chopped coarsely
2 large carrots (360g), chopped coarsely
4 medium tomatoes (600g), chopped coarsely
2 tablespoons tomato paste
1 cup (250ml) dry white wine
1 cup (250ml) beef stock
400g can crushed tomatoes
4 sprigs fresh lemon thyme
½ cup (75g) drained semi-dried tomatoes
¼ cup (60ml) lemon juice
1 tablespoon finely grated lemon rind
½ cup (75g) seeded kalamata olives
gremolata
1 tablespoon finely grated lemon rind
⅓ cup finely chopped fresh flat-leaf parsley
2 cloves garlic, chopped finely

1 Coat veal in flour; shake off excess. Heat oil in large deep saucepan; cook veal, in batches, until browned all over.
2 Melt butter in same pan; cook onion, garlic, celery and carrot, stirring, until vegetables just soften. Stir in fresh tomato, paste, wine, stock, undrained tomatoes and thyme.
3 Return veal to pan, fitting pieces upright in single layer; bring to the boil. Reduce heat; simmer, covered, 1¾ hours. Stir in semi-dried tomatoes; simmer, uncovered, about 30 minutes or until veal is tender.
4 Remove veal from pan; cover to keep warm. Boil sauce, uncovered, 10 minutes or until sauce thickens slightly. Stir in juice, rind and olives.
5 Combine ingredients for gremolata in small bowl; sprinkle on osso buco.

preparation time 30 minutes **cooking time** 2 hours 45 minutes
serves 6
nutritional count per serving 21.4g total fat (6.6g saturated fat); 2855kJ (683 cal); 22.3g carbohydrate; 89.0g protein; 8.1g fibre

Osso buco with caper gremolata

8 pieces veal osso buco (2kg)
2 tablespoons plain flour
¼ cup (60ml) olive oil
1 medium brown onion (150g), chopped coarsely
2 cloves garlic, crushed
3 trimmed celery stalks (300g), chopped coarsely
2 large carrots (360g), chopped coarsely
2 x 400g cans crushed tomatoes
2 tablespoons tomato paste
1 cup (250ml) dry white wine
1 cup (250ml) beef stock
3 sprigs fresh thyme
caper gremolata
1 tablespoon finely grated lemon rind
⅓ cup finely chopped fresh flat-leaf parsley
2 cloves garlic, chopped finely
1 tablespoon drained capers, rinsed, chopped finely

1 Toss veal in flour; shake away excess. Heat 2 tablespoons of the oil in large flameproof casserole dish; cook veal, in batches, until browned all over.
2 Heat remaining oil in same dish; cook onion, garlic, celery and carrot, stirring, until vegetables soften. Stir in undrained tomatoes, tomato paste, wine, stock and thyme.
3 Return veal to dish, fitting pieces upright and tightly together in single layer; bring to the boil. Reduce heat; simmer, covered, 2 hours. Uncover; cook about 30 minutes or until veal is almost falling off the bone.
4 Combine ingredients for caper gremolata in small bowl.
5 Divide veal among serving plates; top with sauce, sprinkle with gremolata. Serve with soft polenta (see page 340), if desired.

preparation time 25 minutes **cooking time** 2 hours 45 minutes
serves 4
nutritional count per serving 19.9g total fat (4.4g saturated fat); 2240kJ (536 cal); 13.2g carbohydrate; 68.7g protein; 5.3g fibre

Braised beef curry with dhal

1 tablespoon peanut oil
2 medium brown onions (300g), chopped coarsely
2 cloves garlic, crushed
1 fresh small red thai chilli, chopped finely
1 tablespoon grated fresh ginger
2 teaspoons garam masala
2 tablespoons ground cumin
2 tablespoons ground coriander
2 teaspoons hot paprika
4 cardamom pods, bruised
3 cinnamon sticks, broken
2 cups (500ml) water
2kg beef chuck steak, diced into 2cm pieces
3 cups (750ml) beef stock
½ cup (125ml) coconut milk
⅓ cup chopped fresh coriander
3 cups (600g) red lentils

1 Heat oil in large saucepan; cook onion, garlic, chilli and ginger, stirring, until onion is soft. Stir in spices; cook, stirring, until fragrant.
2 Gradually stir ¼ cup (60ml) of the water into onion mixture until it forms a paste; cook, stirring, 2 minutes. Add beef; stir to coat in paste.
3 Add stock and the remaining water; bring to the boil. Reduce heat; simmer, covered, stirring occasionally, 1½ hours or until beef is tender.
4 Add coconut milk; simmer, uncovered, about 30 minutes or until thickened slightly. Discard cardamom and cinnamon. Stir in coriander.
5 Meanwhile, cook lentils in medium saucepan of boiling water, uncovered, about 10 minutes or until tender; drain.
6 Serve curry with lentils.

preparation time 15 minutes **cooking time** 2 hours 30 minutes
serves 8
nutritional count per serving 18.5g total fat (8.3g saturated fat); 2516kJ (602 cal); 31.8g carbohydrate; 70.7g protein; 11.3g fibre

Mexican meatballs with guacamole

2 tablespoons vegetable oil
1 medium brown onion (150g), chopped finely
1 clove garlic, crushed
1 teaspoon ground cumin
1 teaspoon ground coriander
½ teaspoon chilli powder
750g beef mince
800g can crushed tomatoes
425g can mexican-style beans
⅓ cup (80g) sour cream
guacamole
2 medium avocados (500g)
1 medium tomato (190g), seeded, chopped finely
1 small red onion (100g), chopped finely
2 teaspoons lemon juice

1 Heat half of the oil in large frying pan; cook onion, garlic and spices, stirring, until onion softens.
2 Combine beef and onion mixture in medium bowl; using hands, roll level tablespoons into balls.
3 Heat remaining oil in same pan; cook meatballs, in batches, until browned all over.
4 Bring tomato and beans to the boil in same pan. Reduce heat; simmer, uncovered, about 5 minutes or until mixture thickens slightly. Return meatballs to pan; simmer, uncovered, about 10 minutes or until meatballs are cooked through.
5 Meanwhile, make guacamole.
6 Serve meatballs topped with guacamole and sour cream. Serve with warm flour tortillas, if desired.
guacamole Mash avocados with fork in medium bowl; stir in tomato, onion and juice.

preparation time 25 minutes **cooking time** 25 minutes
serves 4
nutritional count per serving 49.6g total fat (15.7g saturated fat); 3181kJ (761 cal); 23.3g carbohydrate; 51.2g protein; 10.5g fibre

Beef, barley and mushroom stew

1kg beef chuck steak, diced into 3cm pieces
¼ cup (35g) plain flour
2 tablespoons olive oil
20g butter
2 medium brown onions (300g), chopped finely
3 cloves garlic, crushed
1 medium carrot (120g), chopped finely
1 trimmed celery stalk (100g), chopped finely
4 sprigs fresh thyme
1 sprig fresh rosemary
1 bay leaf
½ cup (100g) pearl barley
2 cups (500ml) beef stock
½ cup (125ml) dry white wine
2 cups (500ml) water
200g swiss brown mushrooms, quartered
200g button mushrooms, quartered

1 Preheat oven to 160°C/140°C fan-forced.
2 Coat beef in flour; shake off excess. Heat oil in large flameproof casserole dish; cook beef, in batches, until browned all over.
3 Melt butter in same dish; cook onion, garlic, carrot, celery and herbs, stirring, until vegetables soften. Add barley, stock, wine and the water; bring to the boil. Return beef to dish, cover; cook in oven 1½ hours.
4 Stir in mushrooms; cook, uncovered, in oven about 30 minutes or until beef and mushrooms are tender.
5 Serve stew with parsnip mash (see page 372) and a few sprigs fresh thyme, if desired.

preparation time 35 minutes **cooking time** 2 hours 20 minutes
serves 4
nutritional count per serving 21.8g total fat (6.3g saturated fat); 2462kJ (589 cal); 28.7g carbohydrate; 60.3g protein; 8.2g fibre

Veal with artichokes, olives and lemon

1 medium unpeeled lemon (140g), chopped coarsely
4 medium globe artichokes (800g)
1.2kg diced veal neck
¼ cup (35g) plain flour
50g butter
¼ cup (60ml) olive oil
1 medium brown onion (150g), chopped finely
1 medium carrot (120g), chopped finely
2 cloves garlic, chopped finely
2 sprigs fresh marjoram
2 sprigs fresh oregano
1 cup (250ml) dry white wine
2 cups (500ml) chicken stock
1 cup (150g) seeded kalamata olives
2 teaspoons finely grated lemon rind
2 tablespoons lemon juice
2 tablespoons fresh oregano leaves
1 medium lemon (140g), cut into six wedges

1 Place chopped lemon in large bowl half-filled with cold water. Discard outer leaves from artichokes; cut tips from remaining leaves. Trim then peel stalks. Quarter artichokes lengthways; using teaspoon, remove and discard chokes. Place in lemon water.
2 Preheat oven to 160°C/140°C fan-forced.
3 Coat veal in flour; shake off excess. Heat butter and 2 tablespoons of the oil in large flameproof casserole dish; cook veal, in batches, until browned all over.
4 Heat remaining oil in same dish; cook onion, carrot, garlic, herb sprigs, stirring, until vegetables soften. Add wine; bring to the boil. Return veal to dish with stock; cook, covered, in oven 1 hour. Add artichokes; cook, covered, in oven 30 minutes. Uncover; cook a further 30 minutes or until veal is tender. Stir in olives, rind and juice.
5 Divide stew among serving plates; top with oregano leaves.

preparation time 40 minutes **cooking time** 2 hours 25 minutes
serves 6
nutritional count per serving 21.6g total fat (7.4g saturated fat); 2040kJ (488 cal); 14.6g carbohydrate; 50.2g protein; 3.4g fibre

Braised oxtail with orange gremolata

1.5kg oxtails, diced into 5cm pieces
2 tablespoons plain flour
2 tablespoons olive oil
1 medium brown onion (150g), chopped coarsely
2 cloves garlic, crushed
½ cup (125ml) sweet sherry
400g can crushed tomatoes
1 cup (250ml) beef stock
1 cup (250ml) water
4 sprigs fresh thyme
2 bay leaves
10cm strip orange rind
4 medium tomatoes (600g), chopped coarsely
orange gremolata
¼ cup finely chopped fresh flat-leaf parsley
1 tablespoon finely grated orange rind
1 clove garlic, crushed

1 Preheat oven to 160°C/140°C fan-forced.
2 Coat oxtail in flour; shake off excess. Heat half of the oil in large flameproof casserole dish; cook oxtail, in batches, until browned all over.
3 Heat remaining oil in same dish; cook onion and garlic, stirring, until onion softens. Return oxtail to dish with sherry, undrained tomatoes, stock, the water, herbs and rind; cook, covered, in oven about 3 hours or until oxtail is tender. Stir in chopped tomato.
4 Meanwhile, combine ingredients for orange gremolata in small bowl.
5 Serve oxtail sprinkled with gremolata on mashed potato (see page 360), if desired.

preparation time 20 minutes **cooking time** 3 hours 15 minutes
serves 4
nutritional count per serving 110.2g total fat (40g saturated fat); 5656kJ (1353 cal); 15.8g carbohydrate; 69.5g protein; 4.1g fibre

153

Chilli con carne with corn dumplings

2 tablespoons olive oil
1.5kg chuck steak, diced into 4cm pieces
2 medium brown onions (300g), chopped
2 cloves garlic, crushed
1 large green capsicum (350g), chopped
2 teaspoons sweet paprika
2 teaspoons ground cumin
2 teaspoons chilli powder
800g can whole peeled tomatoes
2 tablespoons tomato paste
1 cup (250ml) beef stock
400g can red kidney beans, rinsed, drained
corn dumplings
½ cup (75g) self-raising flour
½ cup (85g) polenta
50g butter, chopped
1 egg, beaten lightly
¼ cup (30g) coarsely grated cheddar cheese
¼ cup coarsely chopped fresh coriander
130g can corn kernels, drained
1 tablespoon milk, approximately

1 Heat half the oil in large saucepan; cook steak, in batches, until browned.
2 Heat remaining oil in same pan; cook onion, garlic and capsicum, stirring, until vegetables soften. Add spices; cook, stirring until fragrant.
3 Return steak to pan with undrained tomatoes, paste and stock; bring to the boil. Reduce heat; simmer, covered, for 2½ hours or until tender.
4 Shred a quarter of the steak coarsely with two forks, add meat to pan with kidney beans; bring to the boil. Simmer, uncovered, for 15 minutes.
5 Meanwhile, make corn dumplings. Drop level tablespoons of dumpling mixture, about 2cm apart, on top of steak mixture. Simmer, covered, about 20 minutes or until dumplings are cooked through.
corn dumplings Place flour and polenta in a medium bowl; rub in butter. Stir in egg, cheese, coriander, corn and enough milk for a soft, sticky dough.

preparation time 25 minutes **cooking time** 3 hours 30 minutes
serves 6
nutritional count per serving 28.2g total fat (11.7g saturated fat); 2784kJ (666 cal); 37.0g carbohydrate; 62.1g protein; 7.4g fibre

Beef and red wine casserole

2 cups (500ml) water
1kg beef skirt steak, trimmed, diced into 3cm pieces
2 medium brown onions (300g), sliced thickly
2 tablespoons olive oil
6 cloves garlic, crushed
2 cups (500ml) beef stock
2 cups (500ml) dry red wine
½ cup (140g) tomato paste
1 tablespoon finely chopped fresh rosemary
1 tablespoon finely chopped fresh flat-leaf parsley
500g fresh fettuccine

1 Combine the water, steak, onion, oil, garlic, stock, wine and paste in deep 3 litre (12 cup) microwave-safe dish; cook, covered, on HIGH (100%) for 50 minutes, stirring every 15 minutes to ensure steak remains covered in cooking liquid. Uncover; cook on HIGH (100%) about 10 minutes or until steak is tender. Stir in herbs.
2 During final 10 minutes of casserole cooking time, cook pasta in large saucepan of boiling water, uncovered, until just tender; drain.
3 Divide pasta among serving dishes; top with beef casserole.

preparation time 20 minutes **cooking time** 1 hour
serves 4
nutritional count per serving 16.3g total fat (4.1g saturated fat); 3010kJ (720 cal); 51.5g carbohydrate; 67.5g protein; 5.3g fibre
tip Round steak and chuck steak are also suitable for this recipe.

Beef and prune tagine

2 large red onions (600g), chopped finely
2 tablespoons olive oil
1 teaspoon cracked black pepper
pinch saffron threads
1 teaspoon ground cinnamon
¼ teaspoon ground ginger
1kg beef blade steak, diced into 4cm pieces
50g butter, chopped
425g can diced tomatoes
1 cup (250ml) water
2 tablespoons white sugar
¾ cup (100g) roasted slivered almonds
1½ cups (250g) seeded prunes
1 teaspoon finely grated lemon rind
¼ teaspoon ground cinnamon, extra

1 Combine onion, oil, pepper, saffron, cinnamon and ginger in large bowl, add beef; toss beef to coat in mixture.
2 Place beef in large deep saucepan with butter, undrained tomatoes, the water, half of the sugar and ½ cup of the nuts; bring to the boil. Reduce heat; simmer, covered, 1½ hours. Remove 1 cup cooking liquid; reserve. Simmer tagine, uncovered, 30 minutes.
3 Meanwhile, place prunes in small bowl, cover with boiling water; stand 20 minutes, drain. Place prunes in small saucepan with rind, extra cinnamon, remaining sugar and reserved cooking liquid; bring to the boil. Reduce heat; simmer, uncovered, about 15 minutes or until prunes soften. Stir into tagine.
4 Serve tagine sprinkled with remaining nuts; serve with spinach couscous (see page 347), if desired.

preparation time 25 minutes **cooking time** 2 hours 30 minutes
serves 4
nutritional count per serving 50.0g total fat (15.9g saturated fat); 3683kJ (881 cal); 41.3g carbohydrate; 62.0g protein; 10.3g fibre

Hoisin-braised short ribs

2kg beef short ribs
½ cup (125ml) hoisin sauce
1 cup (250ml) beef stock
¼ cup (55g) firmly packed brown sugar
5cm piece fresh ginger (25g), grated
2 cloves garlic, crushed
2 star anise
½ cup (125ml) orange juice
5cm strip orange rind
1 fresh long red chilli, chopped coarsely

1 Preheat oven to 150°C/130°C fan-forced.
2 Place ribs and combined remaining ingredients in large shallow baking dish; turn ribs to coat in mixture.
3 Cook ribs, covered, in oven 2 hours. Turn ribs; cook, covered, about another 30 minutes or until ribs are tender. Remove ribs from dish; cover to keep warm.
4 Pour braising liquid into large jug; skim fat from surface. Place liquid in medium saucepan; bring to the boil. Reduce heat; simmer, uncovered, about 10 minutes or until sauce thickens slightly.
5 Drizzle ribs with sauce; serve with steamed jasmine rice and choy sum, if desired.

preparation time 10 minutes **cooking time** 2 hours 45 minutes
serves 4
nutritional count per serving 27.6g total fat (11.7g saturated fat); 2780kJ (665 cal); 29.6g carbohydrate; 75.5g protein; 4.2g fibre

Trinidadian beef

2 tablespoons coriander seeds
2 tablespoons cumin seeds
½ teaspoon fennel seeds
½ teaspoon black mustard seeds
½ teaspoon fenugreek seeds
1 teaspoon black peppercorns
1 medium brown onion (150g), chopped finely
2 cloves garlic, quartered
½ teaspoon ground ginger
3 fresh small red thai chillies, chopped coarsely
2 tablespoons coarsely chopped fresh flat-leaf parsley
¼ cup coarsely chopped fresh coriander
1 tablespoon fresh thyme leaves
⅓ cup (80ml) peanut oil
1kg gravy beef, diced into 3cm pieces
3 cloves garlic, extra, crushed
1 tablespoon hot curry powder
3 cups (750ml) beef stock
2 fresh small red thai chillies, extra, sliced thinly

1 Dry-fry seeds and peppercorns in small frying pan, stirring, 1 minute or until fragrant. Crush mixture using mortar and pestle.
2 Blend or process onion, quartered garlic, ginger, chopped chilli, herbs and 1 tablespoon of the oil until mixture forms a paste.
3 Combine paste and beef in large bowl. Cover; refrigerate 30 minutes.
4 Heat remaining oil in large saucepan; cook crushed garlic and curry powder, stirring, 1 minute. Add beef mixture; cook, stirring, over medium heat 10 minutes. Add stock and crushed spice mixture; simmer, covered, 1 hour. Uncover; simmer about 1 hour, stirring occasionally, or until meat is tender and sauce thickens slightly.
5 Serve curry sprinkled with sliced chilli.

preparation time 25 minutes (plus refrigeration time)
cooking time 2 hours 15 minutes **serves** 4
nutritional count per serving 30.2g total fat (8.3g saturated fat);
2111kJ (505 cal); 3.7g carbohydrate; 53.9g protein; 1.9g fibre

Beef and horseradish stew with kumara potato mash

2 tablespoons olive oil
1.5kg beef chuck steak, diced into 5cm pieces
3 medium brown onions (450g), sliced into wedges
3 cloves garlic, crushed
8cm piece fresh ginger (40g), grated
2 teaspoons curry powder
¼ cup (35g) plain flour
3 cups (750ml) beef stock
1 tablespoon worcestershire sauce
2 tablespoons horseradish cream
¼ cup coarsely chopped fresh flat-leaf parsley
kumara potato mash
1kg kumara, chopped coarsely
500g potatoes, chopped coarsely
¾ cup (180ml) cream
50g butter

1 Preheat oven to 140°C/120°C fan-forced.
2 Heat oil in large flameproof casserole dish; cook beef, in batches, until browned.
3 Cook onion, garlic and ginger in same dish, stirring, about 5 minutes or until onion softens. Add curry powder and flour; cook, stirring, 5 minutes.
4 Return beef to dish with stock and sauce; cook, stirring, over heat until mixture boils and thickens. Cook, covered tightly, in oven about 3 hours or until beef is tender, stirring occasionally.
5 Meanwhile, make kumara potato mash.
6 Stir horseradish cream and parsley through beef mixture off the heat just before serving; serve with mash.
kumara potato mash Boil, steam or microwave kumara and potato, separately, until tender; drain. Mash kumara and potato with warmed cream and butter in large bowl until smooth; cover to keep warm.

preparation time 40 minutes **cooking time** 3 hours 30 minutes
serves 6
nutritional count per serving 38.6g total fat (19.3g saturated fat); 3177kJ (760 cal); 41.4g carbohydrate; 59.1g protein; 5.6g fibre

Braciole with cheese

8 beef minute steaks (1.2kg)
4 cloves garlic, crushed
8 slices prosciutto (120g)
200g smoked provolone cheese, cut into 8 slices
¾ cup (50g) stale breadcrumbs
½ cup (75g) plain flour
¼ cup (60ml) olive oil
1 medium white onion (150g), sliced thinly
425g canned tomatoes
2 tablespoons tomato paste
1 cup (250ml) water
¼ cup (60ml) red wine

1 Place beef out flat on clean surface. Spread garlic over each piece. Top each with a slice of prosciutto and a slice of cheese. Place 1 tablespoon of the breadcrumbs in centre of each piece. Roll up beef to enclose filling; secure with kitchen string. Toss rolls in flour; shake away excess.
2 Heat oil in large saucepan; cook beef rolls until browned all over. Remove from pan.
3 Cook onion in same pan, over low heat until very soft. Stir in undrained tomatoes, paste, the water and wine; bring to the boil. Reduce heat; simmer, covered, 20 minutes.
4 Remove lid; return beef rolls to pan. Simmer, uncovered, 15 minutes or until sauce thickens slightly. Remove string before serving.

preparation time 30 minutes **cooking time** 1 hour 45 minutes
serves 4
nutritional count per serving 48.3g total fat (19.3g saturated fat);
3850kJ (921 cal); 28.7g carbohydrate; 88.6g protein; 4.0g fibre

Mexican beans with sausages

1 cup (200g) dried kidney beans
800g beef sausages, chopped coarsely
1 tablespoon olive oil
1 large white onion (200g), chopped coarsely
3 cloves garlic, crushed
1 large red capsicum (350g), chopped coarsely
½ teaspoon ground cumin
2 teaspoons sweet smoked paprika
1 teaspoon dried chilli flakes
2 x 400g cans crushed tomatoes
2 tablespoons coarsely chopped fresh oregano

1 Soak beans in medium bowl of cold water overnight; drain. Rinse under cold water; drain.
2 Place beans in medium saucepan of boiling water; return to the boil. Reduce heat; simmer, uncovered, about 30 minutes or until beans are almost tender. Drain.
3 Cook sausages, in batches, in large deep saucepan until browned; drain on absorbent paper.
4 Heat oil in same pan; cook onion, garlic and capsicum, stirring, until onion softens. Add cumin, paprika and chilli; cook, stirring, about 2 minutes or until fragrant. Add beans and undrained tomatoes; bring to the boil. Reduce heat; simmer, covered, about 1 hour or until beans are tender.
5 Return sausages to pan; simmer, covered, about 10 minutes or until sausages are cooked through. Remove from heat; stir in oregano. Serve with tortillas, if desired.

preparation time 20 minutes (plus standing time)
cooking time 2 hours 15 minutes **serves** 4
nutritional count per serving 56.9g total fat (25.2g saturated fat); 3323kJ (795 cal); 33.5g carbohydrate; 38.1g protein; 20.2g fibre

Veal goulash with braised red cabbage

1 tablespoon olive oil
1 medium brown onion (150g), sliced thickly
1 medium red capsicum (200g), sliced thickly
2 cloves garlic, crushed
800g boneless veal leg, diced into 3cm pieces
1 tablespoon sweet paprika
½ teaspoon cayenne pepper
425g can crushed tomatoes
1½ cups (375ml) beef stock
1 cup (200g) brown long-grain rice
30g butter
400g red cabbage, chopped coarsely

1 Heat oil in large saucepan; cook onion, capsicum and garlic until onion softens. Add veal, paprika, pepper, undrained tomato and ½ cup (125ml) of the stock; bring to the boil, stirring. Reduce heat; simmer, uncovered, about 1 hour or until veal is tender and sauce thickens slightly.
2 Meanwhile, cook rice in medium saucepan of boiling water until just tender; drain.
3 Melt butter in large frying pan; cook cabbage, stirring, about 5 minutes or until just softened. Add remaining stock; bring to the boil. Reduce heat; simmer, covered, 10 minutes.
4 Serve goulash with rice and cabbage.

preparation time 20 minutes **cooking time** 1 hour 30 minutes
serves 4
nutritional count per serving 15.8g total fat (5.8g saturated fat); 2404kJ (575 cal); 49.6g carbohydrate; 54.0g protein; 8.0g fibre

Beef bourguignon

350g shallots
2 tablespoons olive oil
2kg gravy beef, trimmed, chopped coarsely
30g butter
4 rindles bacon rashers (260g), chopped coarsely
400g mushrooms, halved
2 cloves garlic, crushed
¼ cup (35g) plain flour
1¼ cups (310ml) beef stock
2½ cups (625ml) dry red wine
2 bay leaves
2 sprigs fresh thyme
½ cup coarsely chopped fresh flat-leaf parsley

1 Peel shallots, leaving root end intact so shallot remains whole during cooking.
2 Heat oil in large flameproof casserole dish; cook beef, in batches, until browned.
3 Heat butter in same dish; cook shallots, bacon, mushrooms and garlic, stirring, until shallots are browned lightly. Sprinkle flour over mixture; cook, stirring, until flour mixture thickens and bubbles. Gradually add stock and wine; stir over heat until mixture boils and thickens.
4 Return beef and any juices to dish, add bay leaves and thyme; bring to the boil. Reduce heat; simmer, covered, about 2 hours or until beef is tender, stirring every 30 minutes.
5 Stir in parsley; discard bay leaves just before serving.

preparation time 30 minutes **cooking time** 2 hours 30 minutes
serves 6
nutritional count per serving 31.4g total fat (12.1g saturated fat); 2658kJ (636 cal); 6.6g carbohydrate; 80.3g protein; 2.8g fibre

Beef stew with parsley dumplings

1kg beef chuck steak, diced into 5cm pieces
2 tablespoons plain flour
2 tablespoons olive oil
20g butter
2 medium brown onions (300g), chopped coarsely
2 cloves garlic, crushed
2 medium carrots (240g), chopped coarsely
1 cup (250ml) dry red wine
2 tablespoons tomato paste
2 cups (500ml) beef stock
4 sprigs fresh thyme
parsley dumplings
1 cup (150g) self-raising flour
50g butter
1 egg, beaten lightly
¼ cup (20g) coarsely grated parmesan cheese
¼ cup finely chopped fresh flat-leaf parsley
⅓ cup (50g) drained sun-dried tomatoes, chopped finely
¼ cup (60ml) milk

1 Preheat oven to 180°C/160°C fan-forced.
2 Coat beef in flour; shake off excess. Heat oil in large flameproof casserole dish; cook beef, in batches, until browned all over.
3 Melt butter in same dish; cook onion, garlic and carrot, stirring, until vegetables soften. Add wine; cook, stirring, until liquid reduces to ¼ cup. Return beef to dish with paste, stock and thyme; bring to the boil. Cover; cook in oven 1¾ hours.
4 Meanwhile, make parsley dumpling mixture.
5 Drop level tablespoons of the mixture, about 2cm apart, onto top of stew. Cook, uncovered, in oven about 20 minutes or until dumplings are browned lightly and cooked through. Serve with a mixed salad, if desired.
parsley dumplings Place flour in medium bowl; rub in butter. Stir in egg, cheese, parsley, tomato and enough milk to make a soft, sticky dough.

preparation time 20 minutes **cooking time** 2 hours 30 minutes
serves 4
nutritional count per serving 39.7g total fat (17.4g saturated fat); 3457kJ (827 cal); 43.0g carbohydrate; 63.9g protein; 6.7g fibre

Beef stroganoff with fettuccine

2 tablespoons vegetable oil
600g beef rump steak, sliced thinly
1 medium brown onion (150g), sliced thinly
2 cloves garlic, crushed
1 teaspoon sweet paprika
400g swiss brown mushrooms, sliced thickly
375g fettuccine
2 tablespoons dry red wine
1 tablespoon lemon juice
2 tablespoons tomato paste
1¼ cups (300g) sour cream
1 tablespoon coarsely chopped fresh dill

1 Heat half of the oil in large frying pan; cook beef, in batches, until browned lightly.
2 Heat remaining oil in same pan; cook onion and garlic, stirring, until onion softens. Add paprika and mushrooms; cook, stirring, until mushrooms are just tender.
3 Meanwhile, cook pasta in large saucepan of boiling water, uncovered, until just tender. Drain.
4 Return beef to pan with wine and juice; bring to the boil. Reduce heat; simmer, covered, about 5 minutes or until beef is tender. Add paste, sour cream and dill; cook, stirring, until heated through.
5 Serve stroganoff over drained pasta.

preparation time 15 minutes **cooking time** 20 minutes
serves 4
nutritional count per serving 44.3g total fat (22.6g saturated fat); 3787kJ (906 cal); 69.9g carbohydrate; 51.9g protein; 6.8g fibre

Veal with red wine and balsamic vinegar

¼ cup (60ml) olive oil
1kg diced veal shoulder
10 pickling onions (400g), halved
1 medium carrot (120g), chopped finely
1 trimmed celery stalk (100g), chopped finely
2 cloves garlic, chopped finely
4 rindless bacon rashers (260g), chopped coarsely
¼ cup (60ml) balsamic vinegar
2 tablespoons tomato paste
200g mushrooms, quartered
425g can diced tomatoes
1 cup (250ml) dry red wine
1 cup (250ml) beef stock
2 tablespoons coarsely chopped fresh garlic chives

1 Preheat oven to 160°C/140°C fan-forced.
2 Heat 2 tablespoons of the oil in large flameproof casserole dish; cook veal, in batches, until browned all over.
3 Heat remaining oil in same dish; cook onion, carrot, celery, garlic and bacon, stirring, until vegetables soften. Add vinegar and paste; cook, stirring, 2 minutes. Add mushrooms, undrained tomatoes, wine and stock; bring to the boil. Boil, uncovered, 5 minutes.
4 Return veal to dish; cook, covered, in oven about 1½ hours or until veal is tender. Stir in chives.
5 Serve veal with mashed potato (see page 360), if desired.

preparation time 25 minutes **cooking time** 2 hours
serves 4
nutritional count per serving 26.8g total fat (6.2g saturated fat); 2592kJ (620 cal); 8.7g carbohydrate; 73.4g protein; 4.8g fibre

Tuscan beef stew

1 tablespoon olive oil
400g spring onions, trimmed
1kg beef chuck steak, diced into 3cm pieces
30g butter
2 tablespoons plain flour
2 cups (500ml) dry red wine
1 cup (250ml) beef stock
1 cup (250ml) water
2 cloves garlic, crushed
6 sprigs thyme
2 bay leaves
1 trimmed stick celery (100g), chopped coarsely
400g baby carrots, trimmed, halved
2 cups (250g) frozen peas
⅓ cup coarsely chopped fresh flat-leaf parsley

1 Heat oil in large saucepan; cook onions, stirring occasionally, about 10 minutes or until browned lightly. Remove from pan.
2 Cook steak, in batches, over high heat in same pan, until browned all over.
3 Melt butter in same pan, add flour; cook, stirring, until mixture bubbles and thickens. Gradually stir in wine, stock and the water; stir until mixture boils and thickens.
4 Return steak to pan with garlic, thyme and bay leaves; bring to the boil. Reduce heat; simmer, covered, 1½ hours. Add onions, celery and carrot; simmer, covered, 30 minutes. Add peas; simmer, uncovered, until peas are just tender. Stir in parsley just before serving.

preparation time 15 minutes **cooking time** 2 hours 40 minutes
serves 4
nutritional count per serving 22.6g total fat (9.5g saturated fat); 2504kJ (599 cal); 16.4g carbohydrate; 57.4g protein; 9.0g fibre
tip Round steak and skirt steak are also suitable for this recipe.

Beef and barley casserole

2 tablespoons olive oil
1kg beef chuck steak, diced into 3cm cubes
8 pickling onions (320g), halved
2 medium carrots (240g), chopped coarsely
1 cup (250ml) dry red wine
1 cup (250ml) beef stock
2 x 400g cans diced tomatoes
2 sprigs fresh rosemary
7 black peppercorns
200g button mushrooms
½ cup (100g) pearl barley
2 tablespoons fresh oregano leaves

1 Preheat oven to 180°C/160°C fan-forced.
2 Heat half the oil in large flameproof casserole dish; cook beef, in batches, until browned.
3 Heat remaining oil in same dish; cook onion and carrot, stirring, until vegetables soften. Return beef to dish with wine, stock, undrained tomatoes, rosemary and peppercorns; bring to the boil. Cover; cook in oven 2 hours, stirring occasionally.
4 Stir in mushrooms and barley; cook, uncovered, in oven 45 minutes or until barley is tender. Serve sprinkled with oregano.

preparation time 15 minutes **cooking time** 3 hours
serves 4
nutritional count per serving 22.4g total fat (6.3g saturated fat); 2851kJ (682 cal); 43g carbohydrate; 60.5g protein; 11.5g fibre

Osso buco

Ask your butcher to cut the veal shin into fairly thick (about 4cm) pieces.

12 pieces veal osso buco (2.5kg)
¼ cup (35g) plain flour
¼ cup (60ml) olive oil
40g butter
1 medium brown onion (150g), chopped coarsely
2 cloves garlic, crushed
3 trimmed celery stalks (300g), chopped coarsely
2 large carrots (360g), chopped coarsely
4 medium tomatoes (600g), chopped coarsely
2 tablespoons tomato paste
1 cup (250ml) dry white wine
1 cup (250ml) beef stock
400g can crushed tomatoes
3 sprigs fresh thyme
¼ cup coarsely chopped fresh flat-leaf parsley
gremolata
1 tablespoon finely grated lemon rind
⅓ cup finely chopped fresh flat-leaf parsley
2 cloves garlic, chopped finely

1 Coat veal in flour; shake away excess flour. Heat oil in large flameproof casserole dish; cook veal, in batches, until browned.
2 Melt butter in same dish; cook onion, garlic, celery and carrot, stirring, until vegetables soften. Stir in remaining ingredients.
3 Return veal to dish, fitting pieces upright and tightly together in single layer; bring to the boil. Reduce heat; simmer, covered, 1¾ hours. Uncover; cook further 30 minutes.
4 Remove veal from dish; cover to keep warm. Bring sauce to the boil; boil, uncovered, about 10 minutes or until sauce thickens slightly.
5 Meanwhile, combine ingredients for gremolata in small bowl.
6 Divide veal among serving plates; top with sauce, sprinkle with gremolata. Serve with mashed potato or soft polenta (see pages 360 & 340), if desired.

preparation time 45 minutes **cooking time** 2 hours 35 minutes
serves 6
nutritional count per serving 16.2g total fat (5.2g saturated fat); 2057kJ (492 cal); 14.2g carbohydrate; 62.2g protein; 5.8g fibre

Hearty beef stew with red wine and mushrooms

2 tablespoons olive oil
1.5kg beef blade steak, diced into 2cm pieces
1 large brown onion (200g), sliced thickly
2 cloves garlic, crushed
250g mushrooms, quartered
2 trimmed celery stalks (200g), sliced thickly
800g can crushed tomatoes
½ cup (125ml) dry red wine
1½ cups (375ml) beef stock
2 medium potatoes (400g), quartered
2 large carrots (360g), sliced thickly
2 teaspoons coarsely chopped fresh thyme
200g green beans, trimmed
200g yellow beans, trimmed

1 Heat half of the oil in large saucepan; cook steak, in batches, over high heat until browned.
2 Heat remaining oil in same pan; cook onion and garlic, stirring, until onion softens. Add mushrooms and celery; cook, stirring, 3 minutes.
3 Return steak to pan with undrained tomatoes, wine and stock; bring to the boil. Reduce heat; simmer, covered, 2 hours.
4 Add potato and carrot; simmer, covered, about 30 minutes or until steak is tender. Stir in thyme.
5 Meanwhile, boil, steam or microwave beans until just tender; drain.
6 Serve stew with beans and, if desired, a warmed loaf of ciabatta.

preparation time 10 minutes **cooking time** 2 hours 50 minutes
serves 4
nutritional count per serving 32.5g total fat (10.8g saturated fat); 3377kJ (808 cal); 27.3g carbohydrate; 90.3g protein; 11.8g fibre

Green chilli stew

2 tablespoons olive oil
1kg beef chuck steak, diced into 3cm pieces
1 large brown onion (200g), sliced thinly
2 cloves garlic, sliced thinly
2 teaspoons ground cumin
2 fresh long green chillies, sliced thinly
2 cups (500ml) beef stock
1 tablespoon tomato paste
3 large egg tomatoes (270g), chopped coarsely
500g tiny new potatoes, halved
4 small flour tortillas
¼ cup coarsely chopped fresh coriander

1 Heat half of the oil in large flameproof baking dish; cook steak, in batches, stirring, until browned all over.
2 Preheat oven to 180°C/160°C fan-forced.
3 Heat remaining oil in same dish; cook onion, garlic, cumin and chilli, stirring, until onion softens. Add stock and paste; bring to the boil, stirring. Return steak to dish; cook, covered, in oven 45 minutes.
4 Add tomato and potato; cook, covered, in oven 35 minutes. Uncover; cook further 20 minutes.
5 Meanwhile, cut each tortilla into six wedges. Place, in single layer, on oven trays; toast, uncovered, in oven about 8 minutes or until crisp.
6 Stir coriander into stew just before serving with tortilla crisps and, if desired, grilled cobs of corn.

preparation time 15 minutes **cooking time** 1 hour 40 minutes
serves 4
nutritional count per serving 23.4g total fat (6.6g saturated fat); 2604kJ (623 cal); 40.1g carbohydrate; 59.8g protein; 5.6g fibre

Braised oxtail in peanut sauce

2 oxtails (2kg), diced into 5cm pieces
2 tablespoons plain flour
2 tablespoons vegetable oil
1 large brown onion (200g), chopped coarsely
6 cloves garlic, crushed
1 tablespoon ground coriander
1 tablespoon ground cumin
2 star anise
2 fresh long red chillies, halved lengthways
1 litre (4 cups) beef stock
1 litre (4 cups) water
⅔ cup (200g) red curry paste
⅔ cup (90g) roasted unsalted peanuts, chopped coarsely
300g green beans, trimmed, chopped coarsely
2 green onions, sliced thinly

1 Coat oxtail in flour; shake off excess. Heat half the oil in large flameproof casserole dish; cook oxtail, in batches, until browned.
2 Heat remaining oil in same dish; cook onion and garlic, stirring, until onion softens. Add spices and chilli; cook, stirring, until fragrant. Return oxtail to dish with stock and the water; simmer, covered, 2 hours.
3 Strain beef over large bowl; reserve braising liquid, discard solids. Skim fat from braising liquid.
4 Cook paste in same cleaned dish, stirring, until fragrant. Add 1 litre of the reserved braising liquid; bring to the boil. Add oxtail; simmer, uncovered, about 45 minutes or until oxtail is tender.
5 Add nuts and beans to dish; cook, uncovered, about 5 minutes or until beans are tender.
6 Serve curry sprinkled with green onion.

preparation time 30 minutes **cooking time** 3 hours 20 minutes
serves 4
nutritional count per serving 111.7g total fat (36.8g saturated fat); 5626kJ (1346 cal); 15.6g carbohydrate; 70.0g protein; 6.7 g fibre

Chilli marinated beef in coconut curry sauce

1.5kg beef chuck steak, chopped coarsely
40g butter
2 medium red capsicums (400g), chopped finely
2 medium brown onions (300g), chopped finely
½ cup (125ml) beef stock
½ cup (125ml) coconut milk
1 cinnamon stick
5 dried curry leaves
⅓ cup chopped fresh coriander
marinade
⅓ cup (80ml) white vinegar
2 fresh small 5red thai chillies, sliced thinly
2 tablespoons tomato paste
1 tablespoon chopped fresh coriander
2 cloves garlic, crushed
3 cardamom pods, crushed
2 teaspoons cumin seeds
1 teaspoon ground turmeric

1 Combine ingredients for marinade in large bowl.
2 Add beef to marinade; mix well. Cover; refrigerate 3 hours or overnight.
3 Heat half of the butter in large saucepan; cook beef mixture, in batches, until browned.
4 Heat remaining butter in same pan; cook capsicum and onion, stirring, until onion is soft.
5 Return beef to pan; add stock, coconut milk, cinnamon and curry leaves. Simmer, covered, 1 hour, stirring occasionally. Uncover; simmer further 30 minutes or until beef is tender. Discard cinnamon stick; stir in coriander. Serve with steamed or boiled rice, if desired.

preparation time 20 minutes (plus refrigeration time)
cooking time 2 hours **serves** 6
nutritional count per serving 21.3g total fat (12.2g saturated fat); 1822kJ (436 cal); 6.9g carbohydrate; 53.2g protein; 2.2g fibre

Beef, red wine and chilli casserole

50g butter
1.5kg beef chuck steak, diced into 3cm pieces
2 cloves garlic, crushed
3 fresh small red thai chillies, sliced thinly
1 tablespoon dijon mustard
1 large brown onion (200g), sliced thickly
2 medium tomatoes (380g), chopped coarsely
410g can tomato puree
¾ cup (180ml) dry red wine
1 cup (250ml) beef stock
2 tablespoons coarsely chopped fresh flat-leaf parsley

1 Heat butter in large saucepan; cook beef, in batches, until browned.
2 Cook garlic, chilli, mustard and onion in same pan, stirring, until onion softens.
3 Return beef to pan with tomato; cook, stirring, 2 minutes. Add puree, wine and stock; bring to the boil. Reduce heat; simmer, covered, about 1½ hours or until beef is tender, stirring occasionally. Stir in parsley just before serving.
4 Serve casserole with soft polenta (see page 340), if desired.

preparation time 15 minutes **cooking time** 1 hour 45 minutes
serves 4
nutritional count per serving 27.6g total fat (14.0g saturated fat); 2721kJ (651 cal); 10.7g carbohydrate; 80.1g protein; 4.3g fibre

Pot au feu with stuffed cabbage rolls

2 veal shanks (1.5kg)
2 large carrots (360g), chopped coarsely
1 medium leek (350g), chopped coarsely
2 small turnips (300g), chopped coarsely
6 baby onions (150g)
1 bay leaf
3 cups (750ml) chicken stock
1 litre (4 cups) water
1 small savoy cabbage (1.2kg)
250g pork mince
250g chicken mince
1 egg
1 small brown onion (80g), chopped finely
½ cup (50g) packaged breadcrumbs

1 Place veal, carrot, leek, turnip, baby onions, bay leaf, stock and the water in large saucepan; bring to the boil. Reduce heat; simmer, uncovered, about 1½ hours or until veal is tender. Remove veal; when cool enough to handle, remove meat from bones and chop it coarsely.
2 Remove 12 large leaves from cabbage; cook, uncovered, in batches, in large saucepan of boiling water 3 minutes. Drain leaves on absorbent paper. Finely chop enough of the remaining cabbage to make ⅓ cup; reserve remaining cabbage for another use.
3 Meanwhile, using hand combine pork, chicken, egg, onion, breadcrumbs and chopped cabbage in large bowl; divide mixture among cabbage leaves. Roll leaves to enclose filling, secure with toothpicks.
4 Return veal meat to vegetable mixture in pan, add cabbage rolls; bring to the boil. Reduce heat; simmer, uncovered, about 10 minutes or until cabbage rolls are cooked through. Divide cabbage rolls among serving bowls; ladle soup over top.

preparation time 45 minutes **cooking time** 1 hour 45 minutes
serves 6
nutritional count per serving 7.7g total fat (2.4g saturated fat); 1597kJ (382 cal); 16.0g carbohydrate; 57.4g protein; 8.4g fibre

Curried sausages

800g thick beef sausages
20g butter
1 medium brown onion (150g), chopped coarsely
1 tablespoon curry powder
2 teaspoons plain flour
2 large carrots (360g), chopped coarsely
2 trimmed celery stalks (200g), chopped coarsely
500g baby new potatoes, halved
2 cups (500ml) beef stock
1 cup loosely packed fresh flat-leaf parsley leaves

1 Cook sausages, in batches, in heated deep large frying pan until cooked through. Cut each sausage into thirds.
2 Melt butter in same cleaned pan; cook onion, stirring, until soft. Add curry powder and flour; cook, stirring, 2 minutes.
3 Add vegetables and stock; bring to the boil. Reduce heat; simmer, covered, about 15 minutes or until vegetables are tender. Add sausages; simmer, uncovered, until sauce thickens slightly. Stir in parsley.

preparation time 20 minutes **cooking time** 45 minutes
serves 4
nutritional count per serving 55.8g total fat (27.3g saturated fat); 3177kJ (760 cal); 29.8g carbohydrate; 30.1g protein; 12.8g fibre

lamb

Lamb cassoulet

1 cup (200g) dried white beans
150g piece streaky bacon, rind removed, diced into 1cm pieces
500g thin lamb sausages, sliced thickly
1 medium brown onion (150g), chopped finely
2 trimmed celery stalks (200g), chopped finely
2 cloves garlic, crushed
1 sprig fresh rosemary
2 bay leaves
425g can crushed tomatoes
1 ½ cups (375ml) chicken stock
2 cups (140g) stale breadcrumbs
⅓ cup coarsely chopped fresh flat-leaf parsley

1 Place beans in large bowl, cover with water; soak overnight, drain.
Rinse under cold water; drain. Place beans in medium saucepan covered
with boiling water; bring to the boil. Reduce heat; simmer, covered, about
15 minutes or until beans are just tender. Drain.
2 Preheat oven to 160°C/140°C fan-forced.
3 Cook bacon in large flameproof casserole dish over high heat, pressing
down with back of spoon, until browned all over; remove from dish. Cook
sausage in same dish until browned all over; remove from dish.
4 Cook onion, celery and garlic in same dish, stirring, about 5 minutes or
until soft. Add rosemary, bay leaves, undrained tomatoes, stock, beans,
bacon and sausage; bring to the boil. Cover; cook in oven 30 minutes.
Sprinkle with combined breadcrumbs and parsley, return to oven; cook,
covered, for 30 minutes. Uncover; cook about 10 minutes or until top
browns lightly.
5 Serve cassoulet with green salad, if desired.

preparation time 20 minutes (plus standing time)
cooking time 1 hour 40 minutes **serves** 4
nutritional count per serving 34.2g total fat (13.2g saturated fat);
3285kJ (786 cal); 56.7g carbohydrate; 55.7g protein; 14.3g fibre

Maple syrup-glazed lamb shanks

⅓ cup (80ml) pure maple syrup
1 cup (250ml) chicken stock
1 tablespoon dijon mustard
1½ cups (375ml) orange juice
8 french-trimmed lamb shanks (2kg)

1 Combine syrup, stock, mustard and juice in large deep flameproof casserole dish, add lamb; toss lamb to coat in syrup mixture. Bring to the boil then cover tightly. Reduce heat; cook lamb, turning every 20 minutes, about 2 hours or until lamb is tender.
2 Serve with lamb with roast potatoes (see page 368) and wilted baby spinach leaves, if desired.

preparation time 10 minutes **cooking time** 2 hours
serves 4
nutritional count per serving 5.2g total fat (2.4g saturated fat); 1668kJ (399 cal); 25.7g carbohydrate; 61.1g protein; 0.3g fibre

Lamb and split pea curry

1 cup (200g) yellow split peas
1 tablespoon olive oil
600g lamb fillets, diced into 4cm pieces
2 large brown onions (400g), sliced thinly
5cm piece fresh ginger (25g), chopped finely
2 cloves garlic, crushed
2 tablespoons ground coriander
1 tablespoon sweet paprika
½ teaspoon cayenne pepper
200g yogurt
2 medium tomatoes (300g), chopped coarsely
1¾ cups (430ml) chicken stock
⅔ cup (160ml) light coconut cream
150g baby spinach leaves
⅓ cup coarsely chopped fresh coriander

1 Cook split peas in medium saucepan of boiling water, uncovered, until just tender; drain.
2 Meanwhile, heat half of the oil in large saucepan; cook lamb, in batches, stirring, until cooked as desired. Drain on absorbent paper.
3 Heat remaining oil in same pan; cook onion, stirring, about 15 minutes or until caramelised. Add ginger, garlic, ground coriander, paprika and cayenne; cook, stirring, until fragrant. Add yogurt; cook 5 minutes, without boiling, stirring occasionally.
4 Add tomato, stock and coconut cream to pan; bring to the boil. Reduce heat; simmer, uncovered, about 15 minutes or until sauce thickens slightly.
5 Return lamb to pan with split peas and spinach; cook, stirring, until heated through. Remove from heat; stir in fresh coriander.

preparation time 15 minutes **cooking time** 55 minutes
serves 4
nutritional count per serving 19.3g total fat (9.8g saturated fat); 2153kJ (515 cal); 33.5g carbohydrate; 51.7g protein; 8.9g fibre

Slow-cooked lamb shank and bean ragu

½ cup (100g) dried haricot beans
½ cup (100g) dried borlotti beans
8 french-trimmed lamb shanks (2kg)
2 tablespoons plain flour
1 tablespoon olive oil
1 large brown onion (200g), chopped coarsely
1 medium carrot (120g), chopped coarsely
1 trimmed celery stalk (100g), chopped coarsely
1 fresh long red chilli, chopped finely
¼ cup (60ml) balsamic vinegar
425g can crushed tomatoes
8 drained anchovies in oil
½ cup (125ml) dry white wine
1 cup (250ml) water
⅓ cup coarsely chopped fresh flat-leaf parsley

1 Place beans in large bowl, cover with water; stand overnight. Rinse under cold water; drain. Place beans in medium saucepan, cover with boiling water; bring to the boil. Reduce heat; simmer, uncovered, about 15 minutes or until beans are just tender. Drain.
2 Preheat oven to 180°C/160°C fan-forced.
3 Toss lamb in flour; shake away excess. Heat oil in large flameproof casserole dish; cook lamb, in batches, until browned.
4 Cook onion, carrot, celery and chilli in same dish, stirring, 5 minutes or until onion softens.
5 Return lamb to dish with beans, vinegar, undrained tomatoes, anchovies, wine and the water; bring to the boil. Cook ragu, covered, in oven 1 hour, stirring occasionally. Uncover; cook a further 1 hour or until meat is almost falling off the bone. Stir parsley through ragu just before serving.

preparation time 30 minutes (plus standing time)
cooking time 2 hours 30 minutes **serves** 4
nutritional count per serving 18.1g total fat (6.5g saturated fat); 2077kJ (497 cal); 24.0g carbohydrate; 54.9g protein; 5.2g fibre

Lamb chops with barley, mint and cumin

1 tablespoon olive oil
8 lamb forequarter chops (1.5kg)
20g butter
1 large brown onion (200g), chopped coarsely
2 cloves garlic, chopped finely
1 tablespoon ground cumin
2 large red capsicums (700g), chopped coarsely
1 cup (200g) pearl barley
2 teaspoons finely grated orange rind
1 cup (250ml) orange juice
1 litre (4 cups) chicken stock
2 cups (500ml) water
¼ cup firmly packed fresh mint leaves

1 Heat oil in large deep saucepan; cook lamb, in batches, until browned all over.
2 Heat butter in same pan; cook onion and garlic, stirring, until onion softens. Add cumin and capsicum; cook, stirring, until fragrant.
3 Return lamb to pan with barley, rind, juice, stock and the water; bring to the boil. Reduce heat; simmer, covered, 45 minutes. Uncover; simmer about 30 minutes or until lamb is tender. Strain mixture over large bowl; cover lamb mixture to keep warm.
4 Return cooking liquid to pan; bring to the boil. Boil, uncovered, stirring occasionally, about 15 minutes or until sauce thickens slightly.
5 Divide lamb mixture among serving plates; top with thickened sauce then sprinkle with mint.

preparation time 20 minutes **cooking time** 1 hour 55 minutes
serves 4
nutritional count per serving 28.5g total fat (12.2g saturated fat); 3031kJ (725 cal); 45.7g carbohydrate; 70.9g protein; 8.9g fibre

Braised lamb and yogurt

1 medium brown onion (150g), chopped coarsely
1 tablespoon grated fresh ginger
2 cloves garlic, crushed
1 teaspoon coriander seeds
1 teaspoon cumin seeds
½ teaspoon cardamom seeds
2 tablespoons lime juice
1.5kg boned leg of lamb, chopped coarsely
30g butter
¼ teaspoon cayenne pepper
2 teaspoons ground turmeric
1 teaspoon garam masala
⅔ cup (190g) plain yogurt
⅔ cup (160ml) cream
1 cup (250ml) water
400g can chickpeas, rinsed, drained
2 medium tomatoes (380g), chopped coarsely
1 tablespoon plain flour
2 tablespoons water, extra
¼ cup chopped fresh flat-leaf parsley

1 Blend or process onion, ginger, garlic, seeds and juice until well combined. Combine blended mixture and lamb in medium bowl until lamb is well coated. Cover; refrigerate 3 hours or overnight.
2 Heat butter in large saucepan; stir in cayenne, turmeric and garam masala over medium heat 1 minute.
3 Stir in yogurt, then lamb mixture; cook, stirring, over high heat until lamb is well browned. Stir in combined cream and the water; bring to the boil. Reduce heat; simmer, uncovered, about 1 hour or until lamb is tender. Stir in chickpeas and tomato.
4 Stir in blended flour and the extra water; stir over high heat until sauce boils and thickens. Stir in parsley; serve with lime wedges, if desired.

preparation time 20 minutes (plus refrigeration time)
cooking time 1 hour 15 minutes **serves** 6
nutritional count per serving 31.2g total fat (17.2g saturated fat); 2420kJ (579 cal); 12.0g carbohydrate; 61.2g protein; 3.4g fibre

Lamb shank stew

8 french-trimmed lamb shanks (2kg)
8 cloves garlic, halved
2 medium lemons (280g)
2 tablespoons olive oil
3 large brown onions (600g), chopped coarsely
2 cups (500ml) dry red wine
3 medium carrots (360g), quartered lengthways
3 trimmed celery stalks (300g), chopped coarsely
4 bay leaves
8 sprigs fresh thyme
1.75 litres (7 cups) chicken stock
½ cup finely chopped fresh flat-leaf parsley
¼ cup finely chopped fresh mint

1 Pierce meatiest part of each shank in two places with sharp knife; press garlic into cuts. Grate rind of both lemons finely; reserve. Halve lemons; rub cut sides all over shanks.
2 Preheat oven to 180°C/160°C fan-forced.
3 Heat oil in large flameproof casserole dish; cook shanks, in batches, until browned.
4 Cook onion, stirring, in same dish until softened. Add wine; bring to the boil, then remove dish from heat.
5 Place carrot, celery and shanks, in alternate layers, on onion mixture in dish. Top with bay leaves and thyme; carefully pour stock over the top. Cover dish tightly with lid or foil; cook in oven about 3 hours or until meat is tender.
6 Meanwhile, combine reserved rind, parsley and mint in small bowl.
7 Transfer shanks to platter; cover to keep warm. Strain pan juices through a sieve into medium saucepan; discard solids. Boil pan juices, uncovered, stirring occasionally, until reduced by half.
8 Serve shanks sprinkled with lemon-herb mixture, drizzle with pan juices. Serve with mashed potato (see page 360) and steamed green beans, if desired.

preparation time 20 minutes **cooking time** 3 hours 20 minutes
serves 8
nutritional count per serving 3.5g total fat (1.6g saturated fat); 1062kJ (254 cal); 8.7g carbohydrate; 34.4g protein; 3.5g fibre

Lamb biryani

1.5kg boneless lamb shoulder, diced into 2cm pieces
5cm piece fresh ginger (25g), grated finely
3 cloves garlic, crushed
2 fresh small red chillies, chopped finely
3 teaspoons garam masala
¼ teaspoon ground turmeric
½ teaspoon ground chilli powder
1 cup (280g) thick yogurt
50g butter
3 large brown onions (600g), sliced thickly
1 cup (250ml) beef stock
2 cups (400g) basmati rice, washed, drained
1 cup (140g) flaked almonds
⅓ cup (55g) sultanas
pinch saffron threads
2 tablespoons hot milk
¼ cup fresh coriander leaves

1 Combine lamb, ginger, garlic, chillies, garam masala, turmeric, chilli powder and yogurt in large bowl. Cover; refrigerate overnight.
2 Heat butter in large saucepan; cook onion, covered, about 5 minutes or until onion is soft. Uncover, cook a further 5 minutes or until onions are lightly browned. Remove half of the onion mixture from pan.
3 Add lamb mixture to pan; cook, stirring, until lamb is browned lightly. Add stock; bring to the boil. Simmer, covered, stirring occasionally, 1 hour. Uncover, simmer, for further 30 minutes or until lamb is tender.
4 Meanwhile, cook rice, uncovered, in large saucepan of boiling water 5 minutes; drain. Combine rice, almonds and sultanas in small bowl.
5 Combine the saffron and milk in a small bowl, stand for 15 minutes.
6 Preheat the oven to 180°C/160°C fan-forced.
7 Spread half the lamb mixture into a oiled 3 litre (12-cup) ovenproof dish; top with half of the rice mixture, then remaining lamb and rice. Drizzle saffron mixture over rice, cover with foil; cook in oven 40 minutes or until rice is tender. Serve topped with reheated reserved onions and coriander.

preparation time 35 minutes (plus refrigeration time)
cooking time 2 hours 30 minutes **serves** 8
nutritional count per serving 33.3g total fat (12.7g saturated fat); 2930kJ (701 cal); 51.9g carbohydrate; 46.6g protein; 3.5g fibre

Persian lamb and rhubarb stew

40g butter
1kg diced lamb
1 medium brown onion (150g), sliced thinly
¼ teaspoon saffron threads
½ teaspoon ground cinnamon
¼ teaspoon ground turmeric
2 tablespoons tomato paste
1 cup (250ml) water
2 cups (500ml) chicken stock
2¾ cups (300g) coarsely chopped rhubarb
¼ cup finely chopped fresh mint

1 Melt half of the butter in large deep saucepan; cook lamb, in batches, until browned all over.
2 Melt remaining butter in same pan; cook onion, stirring, until softened. Add spices; cook, stirring, until fragrant. Add paste, the water and stock; bring to the boil. Return lamb to pan, reduce heat; simmer, covered, 1 hour 20 minutes, stirring occasionally.
3 Uncover; simmer about 20 minutes or until lamb is tender. Add rhubarb; simmer, uncovered, about 10 minutes or until rhubarb has softened.
4 Stir mint into stew off the heat; serve with couscous and kalamata olives, if desired.

preparation time 20 minutes **cooking time** 2 hours 10 minutes
serves 4
nutritional count per serving 30.9g total fat (15.7g saturated fat); 2165kJ (518 cal); 3.5g carbohydrate; 55.3g protein; 3.1g fibre

Anchovy and chilli lamb neck chops

8 lamb neck chops (1.4kg), trimmed
4 drained anchovy fillets, chopped finely
2 fresh small red thai chillies, chopped finely
4 cloves garlic, crushed
½ cup (125ml) dry red wine
2 tablespoons olive oil
1 medium brown onion (150g), chopped coarsely
1 tablespoon plain flour
400g can crushed tomatoes
2 cups (500ml) beef stock
¼ cup chopped fresh flat-leaf parsley

1 Combine lamb, anchovy, chilli, garlic and wine in medium bowl. Cover; refrigerate 3 hours or overnight.
2 Preheat oven to 160°C/140°C fan-forced.
3 Heat half of the oil in deep medium baking dish; cook undrained lamb mixture, in batches, until browned all over.
4 Heat remaining oil in same dish; cook onion, stirring, until softened. Add flour; cook, stirring, about 5 minutes or until mixture browns lightly.
5 Return lamb to dish with undrained tomatoes and stock, cover; cook in oven 1½ hours. Uncover, skim fat from surface; cook, turning lamb occasionally, in oven about a further 30 minutes or until lamb is tender.
6 Divide chops among serving plates, sprinkle with parsley; serve with soft polenta (see page 340), if desired.

preparation time 20 minutes (plus refrigeration time)
cooking time 2 hours 25 minutes **serves** 4
nutritional count per serving 44.4g total fat (17.2g saturated fat); 2880kJ (689 cal); 8.3g carbohydrate; 58.3g protein; 2.5g fibre

Lamb and quince tagine with pistachio couscous

40g butter
600g diced lamb
1 medium red onion (170g), chopped coarsely
2 cloves garlic, crushed
1 cinnamon stick
2 teaspoons ground coriander
1 teaspoon ground cumin
1 teaspoon ground ginger
1 teaspoon dried chilli flakes
1½ cups (375ml) water
425g can crushed tomatoes
2 medium quinces (600g), quartered
1 large green zucchini (150g), chopped coarsely
2 tablespoons coarsely chopped fresh coriander
pistachio couscous
1½ cups (300g) couscous
1 cup (250ml) boiling water
20g butter, softened
½ cup finely chopped fresh coriander
¼ cup (35g) roasted shelled pistachios, chopped coarsely

1 Melt butter in large saucepan; cook lamb, in batches, until browned.
2 Cook onion in same pan, stirring, until softened. Add garlic, cinnamon, coriander, cumin, ginger and chilli; cook, stirring, until mixture is fragrant.
3 Return lamb to pan. Stir in water, undrained tomatoes and quince; bring to the boil. Reduce heat; simmer, covered, 30 minutes. Uncover; simmer, stirring occasionally, 1 hour or until quince is tender and sauce thickens.
4 Add zucchini; cook, stirring, 10 minutes or until zucchini is just tender.
5 Meanwhile, make couscous; serve with tagine, sprinkled with coriander.
pistachio couscous Combine couscous with the water and butter in large heatproof bowl. Cover; stand 5 minutes or until water is absorbed, fluffing with fork occasionally. Stir in coriander and nuts.

preparation time 20 minutes **cooking time** 1 hour 30 minutes
serves 4
nutritional count per serving 31g total fat (14.7g saturated fat); 3214kJ (769 cal); 76.7g carbohydrate; 45.4g protein; 12.3g fibre

Lamb shanks with caramelised onion

1 tablespoon olive oil
8 french-trimmed lamb shanks (2kg)
1 tablespoon white sugar
1½ cups (375ml) dry red wine
2 cups (500ml) beef stock
3 cloves garlic, crushed
20g butter
1 small brown onion (80g), chopped finely
1 trimmed celery stalk (100g), chopped finely
1 tablespoon plain flour
1 tablespoon tomato paste
1 tablespoon coarsely chopped fresh rosemary
caramelised onion
40g butter
2 medium red onions (340g), sliced thinly
¼ cup (50g) brown sugar
¼ cup (60ml) raspberry vinegar

1 Preheat oven to 150°C/130°C fan-forced.
2 Heat oil in large flameproof baking dish; cook lamb over heat until browned all over. Stir in sugar, wine, stock and garlic; bring to the boil. Roast lamb, covered, in oven, about 4 hours, turning twice during cooking.
3 Meanwhile, make caramelised onion.
4 Remove lamb from dish; cover to keep warm. Pour pan liquids into large heatproof jug. Return dish to heat, melt butter; cook onion and celery, stirring, until celery is just tender. Stir in flour; cook, stirring, 2 minutes. Add reserved pan liquids, paste and rosemary; bring to the boil. Simmer, uncovered, stirring, about 10 minutes or until it boils and thickens; strain wine sauce into large jug.
5 Serve lamb with wine sauce and caramelised onion, accompanied with a white bean puree, if desired.
caramelised onion Melt butter in medium saucepan; cook onion, stirring, about 15 minutes or until browned and soft. Stir in sugar and vinegar; cook, stirring, about 15 minutes or until onion is caramelised.

preparation time 20 minutes **cooking time** 4 hours 30 minutes
serves 4
nutritional count per serving 32.6g total fat (15.9g saturated fat); 2968kJ (710 cal); 25.9g carbohydrate; 61.5g protein; 2.3g fibre

Lamb and okra in rich tomato sauce with garlic confit

1 tablespoon olive oil
1kg boned lamb shoulder, trimmed, chopped coarsely
2 medium brown onions (300g), chopped coarsely
7 medium tomatoes (1kg), chopped coarsely
1 litre (4 cups) water
200g okra
½ cup loosely packed fresh mint leaves
garlic confit
1 teaspoon coriander seeds
½ teaspoon cardamom seeds
30g butter
5 cloves garlic, sliced thinly
1 teaspoon dried chilli flakes
1 teaspoon salt

1 Heat oil in large deep saucepan; cook lamb, in batches, until browned all over.
2 Cook onion in same pan, stirring, until soft. Add tomato and the water; bring to the boil. Return lamb to pan, reduce heat; simmer, uncovered, stirring occasionally, about 1¾ hours or until lamb is tender.
3 Add okra to lamb mixture; simmer, uncovered, about 15 minutes or until okra is tender.
4 Meanwhile, make garlic confit.
5 Serve casserole with garlic confit, mint and steamed rice, if desired.
garlic confit Crush seeds in mortar and pestle. Melt butter in small saucepan; cook seeds, garlic, chilli and salt over low heat, stirring, about 10 minutes or until garlic softens.

preparation time 20 minutes **cooking time** 2 hours 10 minutes
serves 4
nutritional count per serving 33.5g total fat (15.0g saturated fat); 2286kJ (547 cal); 8.0g carbohydrate; 53.4g protein; 6.4g fibre

Lamb stoba

2 tablespoons vegetable oil
1kg lamb shoulder, trimmed, diced into 3cm pieces
2 medium brown onions (300g), sliced thinly
3cm piece fresh ginger (15g), sliced thinly
2 fresh long red chillies, sliced thinly
1 medium red capsicum (200g), chopped coarsely
2 teaspoons ground cumin
2 teaspoons ground allspice
1 cinnamon stick
2 x 400g cans chopped tomatoes
2 teaspoons finely grated lime rind
2 tablespoons lime juice
¼ cup (55g) firmly packed brown sugar

1 Heat half the oil in large saucepan; cook lamb, in batches, until browned all over.
2 Heat remaining oil in same pan; cook onion, ginger, chilli, capsicum and spices, stirring, until onion softens.
3 Return lamb to pan, add remaining ingredients; simmer, covered, about 1 hour or until lamb is tender.

preparation time 10 minutes **cooking time** 1 hour 30 minutes
serves 4
nutritional count per serving 31.8g total fat (11.2g saturated fat); 2567kJ (614 cal); 24.4g carbohydrate; 55.8g protein; 4.1g fibre

Slow-cooked thai lamb shanks

2 star anise
2 teaspoons ground coriander
⅓ cup (100g) tamarind concentrate
2 tablespoons brown sugar
8cm piece fresh ginger (40g), sliced thinly
1 tablespoon finely chopped lemon grass
1 fresh small red thai chilli, sliced thinly
2 cloves garlic, sliced thinly
1 tablespoon kecap manis
1 cup (250ml) water
8 french-trimmed lamb shanks (2kg)
500g choy sum, chopped into 10cm lengths

1 Preheat oven to 180°C/160°C fan-forced.
2 Dry-fry star anise and coriander in small heated frying pan, stirring, until fragrant. Combine spices with tamarind, sugar, ginger, lemon grass, chilli, garlic, kecap manis and the water in medium jug.
3 Place lamb, in single layer, in large shallow baking dish; drizzle with tamarind mixture. Cook, covered, in the oven, about 2 hours or until meat is almost falling off the bone, turning occasionally.
4 Remove lamb from dish; cover to keep warm. Skim away excess fat from pan juices then strain into small saucepan. Bring to the boil; boil, uncovered, 5 minutes.
5 Steam choy sum until just tender then divide among serving plates. Top with lamb; drizzle with sauce.

preparation time 30 minutes **cooking time** 2 hours 15 minutes
serves 4
nutritional count per serving 12.5g total fat (5.6g saturated fat); 1492kJ (357 cal); 11.7g carbohydrate; 48.1g protein; 2.6g fibre

Madras curry

Backstrap is sold as eye of loin by some butchers.

500g butternut pumpkin, cut into 2cm cubes
200g green beans, chopped coarsely
2 tablespoons vegetable oil
600g lamb backstrap, diced into 2cm pieces
1 medium brown onion (150g), chopped finely
2 cloves garlic, crushed
½ cup (150g) madras curry paste
1 cup (250ml) beef stock
425g can crushed tomatoes
2 cups (400g) basmati rice
1 cup (250ml) buttermilk
½ cup coarsely chopped fresh coriander

1 Boil, steam or microwave pumpkin and beans, separately, until just tender; drain. Rinse beans under cold water; drain.

2 Meanwhile, heat half of the oil in wok; stir-fry lamb, in batches, until just browned.

3 Heat remaining oil in same wok; stir-fry onion and garlic until onion softens. Add paste; stir-fry until fragrant. Return lamb to wok with stock and undrained tomatoes; bring to the boil. Add pumpkin, reduce heat; simmer, covered, 10 minutes, stirring occasionally.

4 Meanwhile, cook rice in large saucepan of boiling water, uncovered, until just tender; drain.

5 Add beans and buttermilk to curry; stir over low heat until heated through. Remove from heat; stir in coriander.

6 Serve curry with rice, sprinkle with extra chopped coriander, if desired.

preparation time 10 minutes **cooking time** 30 minutes
serves 4
nutritional count per serving 36.9g total fat (9.7g saturated fat); 3829kJ (916 cal); 97.4g carbohydrate; 47.9g protein; 9.1g fibre

Lamb with madeira and olive sauce

1 teaspoon vegetable oil
8 french-trimmed lamb shanks (2kg)
4 medium brown onions (600g), chopped finely
8 cloves garlic, peeled
¼ cup (30g) seeded black olives, quartered
2 tablespoons tomato paste
6 medium egg tomatoes (450g), halved
1 cup (250ml) beef stock
½ cup (125ml) madeira
2 teaspoons chopped rosemary

1 Preheat oven to 180°C/160°C fan-forced.
2 Heat oil in 3 litre (12-cup) flameproof casserole dish; cook lamb, in batches, until browned all over.
3 Cook onion and garlic in same dish, stirring, until onion is soft.
4 Return lamb to dish with olives, paste, tomatoes, stock, madeira and rosemary; cook, uncovered, in oven about 1½ hours or until lamb is tender.

preparation time 15 minutes **cooking time** 1 hour 45 minutes
serves 4
nutritional count per serving 6.7g total fat (2.5g saturated fat); 2023kJ (484 cal); 26.5g carbohydrate; 64.5g protein; 4.9g fibre

Lamb shanks with risoni and tomato

8 french-trimmed lamb shanks (2kg)
½ cup (75g) plain flour
2 tablespoons olive oil
4 cloves garlic, crushed
½ cup (125ml) white wine
400g can diced tomatoes
2 tablespoons tomato paste
1 litre (4 cups) chicken stock
1 cup (220g) risoni pasta
3 small zucchini (270g), chopped coarsely
½ cup coarsely chopped fresh flat-leaf parsley
1 teaspoon finely grated lemon rind

1 Preheat oven to 160°C/140°C fan-forced.
2 Toss lamb in flour, shake away excess flour. Heat oil in a large flameproof baking dish; cook lamb until well browned all over.
3 Add garlic to dish, cook until fragrant. Add wine; bring to the boil; simmer until almost evaporated. Stir in tomatoes, paste and stock; bring to the boil. Cover dish tightly with foil; cook in oven 2 hours.
4 Add risoni and zucchini to dish; cook, covered, a further 40 minutes or until tender. Stir in parsley and rind.

preparation time 15 minutes **cooking time** 2 hours 50 minutes
serves 4
nutritional count per serving 16.5g total fat (4.3g saturated fat); 3005kJ (719 cal); 59.7g carbohydrate; 74.0g protein; 5.8g fibre

237

Rogan josh

1kg boned leg of lamb, trimmed, diced into 3cm pieces
2 teaspoons ground cardamom
2 teaspoons ground cumin
2 teaspoons ground coriander
2 tablespoons oil
2 medium brown onions (300g), sliced thinly
4cm piece fresh ginger (20g), grated
4 cloves garlic, crushed
2 teaspoons sweet paprika
½ teaspoon cayenne pepper
½ cup (125ml) beef stock
425g can crushed tomatoes
2 bay leaves
2 cinnamon sticks
200g yogurt
¾ cup (110g) roasted slivered almonds
1 fresh long red chilli, sliced thinly

1 Combine lamb, cardamom, cumin and coriander in medium bowl.
2 Heat half of the oil in large deep saucepan; cook lamb mixture, in batches, until browned all over.
3 Heat remaining oil in same pan; cook onion, ginger, garlic, paprika and cayenne over low heat, stirring, until onion softens.
4 Return lamb to pan with stock, undrained tomatoes, bay leaves and cinnamon. Add yogurt, 1 tablespoon at a time, stirring well between each addition; bring to the boil. Reduce heat; simmer, covered, about 1½ hours or until lamb is tender.
5 Sprinkle lamb with nuts and chilli off the heat; serve with yogurt and naan bread, if desired.

preparation time 20 minutes **cooking time** 2 hours
serves 4
nutritional count per serving 33.8g total fat (6.4g saturated fat); 2617kJ (626 cal); 12.2g carbohydrate; 65.7g protein; 5.3g fibre

Moroccan lamb shanks

8 french-trimmed lamb shanks (2kg)
2 tablespoons plain flour
¼ cup (60ml) olive oil
2 medium brown onions (300g), chopped coarsely
3 cloves garlic, crushed
1 teaspoon ground cinnamon
2 teaspoons ground cumin
2 teaspoons ground coriander
1 cup (250ml) dry red wine
1 litre (4 cups) chicken stock
2 tablespoons honey
2 small kumara (500g), chopped coarsely

1 Preheat oven to 180°C/160°C fan-forced.
2 Toss lamb in flour; shake away excess. Heat 2 tablespoons of the oil in large flameproof casserole dish; cook lamb, in batches, until browned all over, drain on absorbent paper.
3 Heat remaining oil in same dish; cook onion, garlic, cinnamon, cumin and coriander, stirring, until onion softens and mixture is fragrant. Add wine; bring to the boil. Reduce heat; simmer, uncovered, about 5 minutes or until liquid reduces by half.
4 Add stock and honey to same dish; bring to the boil. Return lamb to casserole dish; cook, covered, in oven about 1 hour 30 minutes, turning shanks occasionally. Uncover dish, add kumara; cook, uncovered, about 50 minutes or until kumara is just tender and lamb is almost falling off the bone. Transfer lamb and kumara to platter; cover to keep warm.
5 Place dish with pan juices over high heat; bring to the boil. Boil, uncovered, about 15 minutes or until sauce thickens slightly.
6 Serve shanks with couscous, if desired.

preparation time 15 minutes **cooking time** 2 hours 55 minutes
serves 4
nutritional count per serving 19.7g total fat (4.7g saturated fat); 2679kJ (641 cal); 36.8g carbohydrate; 66.5g protein; 3.5g fibre

Navarin of lamb

2 tablespoons olive oil
8 lamb chump chops (880g)
1 medium brown onion (150g), sliced thinly
3 cloves garlic, crushed
2 tablespoons plain flour
2 cups (500ml) vegetable stock
2 cups (500ml) water
2 x 400g cans diced tomatoes
½ teaspoon black peppercorns
2 bay leaves
1 sprig fresh rosemary
8 baby new potatoes (320g), halved
3 small brown onions (240g), quartered
1 bunch baby turnips (500g), trimmed, peeled, quartered
10 baby carrots (200g), halved lengthways
1 cup (120g) frozen peas
½ cup coarsely chopped fresh flat-leaf parsley

1 Heat oil in large heavy-based saucepan; cook chops, in batches, until browned.
2 Cook sliced onion in same pan, stirring, until just softened. Add garlic and flour; stir until mixture bubbles and thickens. Gradually add stock and the water; stir until mixture boils and thickens slightly.
3 Return chops to pan with undrained tomatoes, peppercorns, bay leaves and rosemary; bring to the boil. Reduce heat; simmer, covered, 20 minutes.
4 Add potatoes, quartered onion, turnip and carrot to pan; simmer, covered, 30 minutes, stirring occasionally. Add peas; simmer, uncovered, until peas are just tender.
5 Sprinkle parsley over navarin just before serving.

preparation time 30 minutes **cooking time** 1 hour 15 minutes
serves 4
nutritional count per serving 37.2g total fat (13.7g saturated fat); 2721kJ (651 cal); 35.5g carbohydrate; 43.3g protein; 11.9g fibre

Neck chop and lentil stew with kumara and carrot mash

1 cup (200g) brown lentils
1 tablespoon vegetable oil
1.5kg lamb neck chops
2 medium brown onions (300g), chopped coarsely
2 cloves garlic, crushed
4 rindless bacon rashers (260g), chopped coarsely
1 teaspoon caraway seeds
2 teaspoons ground cumin
½ cup (125ml) dry red wine
⅓ cup (90g) tomato paste
2 cups (500ml) beef stock
425g can diced tomatoes
½ cup coarsely chopped fresh coriander
kumara and carrot mash
2 medium kumara (800g), chopped coarsely
2 medium carrots (240g), chopped coarsely
1 teaspoon ground cumin
⅓ cup (80ml) buttermilk

1 Cook lentils in large saucepan of boiling water, uncovered, 15 minutes or until tender; drain.
2 Preheat oven to 180°C/160°C fan-forced.
3 Meanwhile, heat oil in large flameproof casserole dish; cook chops, in batches, until browned.
4 Cook onion, garlic and bacon in same pan, stirring, until onion is just browned and bacon is crisp. Add spices; cook, stirring, until fragrant. Add wine, paste, stock and undrained tomatoes; bring to the boil. Return chops to dish, stir in lentils; cook, covered, in oven 1 hour 10 minutes.
5 Meanwhile, make kumara and carrot mash.
6 Stir coriander into stew just before serving with mash.
kumara and carrot mash Boil, steam or microwave kumara and carrot, separately, until tender; drain. Dry-fry cumin in small frying pan until fragrant. Mash vegetables in large bowl with cumin and buttermilk until smooth.

preparation time 20 minutes **cooking time** 1 hour 45 minutes **serves** 4
nutritional count per serving 47.9g total fat (19.6g saturated fat); 3896kJ (932 cal); 44.2g carbohydrate; 76.1g protein; 9.9g fibre

Slow-roasted lamb shanks with anchovies and tomato

125g drained semi-dried tomatoes
8 drained anchovy fillets
1 tablespoon drained capers
4 french-trimmed lamb shanks (1kg)
8 medium potatoes (1.6kg), quartered
800g can whole tomatoes
1 tablespoon extra virgin olive oil

1 Preheat the oven to 150°C/130°C fan-forced.
2 Blend or process semi-dried tomatoes, anchovies and capers to a paste.
3 Pierce meatiest part of each shank in two places with sharp knife; place shanks in deep ovenproof dish. Press half of the paste into slits; spread remaining paste all over shanks.
4 Place potatoes around shanks; pour undrained chopped tomatoes over the lamb and potatoes. Drizzle with oil. Cover with foil; bake in oven for 2½ hours, turning the lamb halfway through cooking time. Remove foil; bake a further 30 minutes or until the lamb is tender
5 Serve with steamed green vegetables; if desired.

preparation time 20 minutes **cooking time** 3 hours
serves 4
nutritional count per serving 10.7g total fat (2.2g saturated fat); 2240kJ (536 cal); 59.1g carbohydrate; 44.2g protein; 12.0g fibre

Chinese spiced lamb shanks

1 fresh long red chilli, chopped finely
1 teaspoon sichuan peppercorns, crushed
2 star anise
¼ cup (60ml) soy sauce
2 tablespoons oyster sauce
½ cup (125ml) orange juice
2 tablespoons honey
2 cloves garlic, chopped coarsely
1 cup (250ml) boiling water
8 french-trimmed lamb shanks (2kg)
500g choy sum, chopped into 10cm lengths
350g gai lan, trimmed

1 Preheat oven to 180°C/160°C fan-forced.
2 Combine chilli, spices, sauces, juice, honey, garlic and the water in medium jug.
3 Place lamb, in single layer, in large shallow baking dish; drizzle with sauce. Cook, covered, in oven, turning lamb occasionally, about 2 hours or until meat is almost falling off the bone.
4 Remove lamb from dish; cover to keep warm. Skim away excess fat; strain sauce into small saucepan. Bring sauce to the boil; boil, uncovered, 2 minutes.
5 Boil, steam or microwave choy sum and gai lan, separately, until tender; drain. Divide vegetables among serving plates; serve with lamb, drizzle with sauce.

preparation time 20 minutes **cooking time** 2 hours 10 minutes
serves 4
nutritional count per serving 5.4g total fat (2.3g saturated fat); 1634kJ (391 cal); 19.4g carbohydrate; 63.5g protein; 3.1g fibre

Lamb and apricot tagine

1⅔ cups (250g) dried apricots
¾ cup (180ml) orange juice
½ cup (125ml) boiling water
2 tablespoons olive oil
900g lamb steaks, chopped coarsely
2 medium red capsicums (400g), chopped coarsely
1 large brown onion (200g), chopped coarsely
2 medium kumara (800g), chopped coarsely
3 cloves garlic, crushed
1 teaspoon ground cinnamon
2 teaspoons ground cumin
2 teaspoons ground coriander
1 cup (250ml) dry red wine
1 litre (4 cups) chicken stock
2 tablespoons honey
1 cup loosely packed fresh coriander leaves
200g yogurt

1 Place apricots, juice and the water in small bowl. Cover; stand 45 minutes.
2 Meanwhile, heat half of the oil in large saucepan; cook lamb, in batches, until browned all over.
3 Heat remaining oil in same pan; cook capsicum, onion, kumara, garlic and ground spices, stirring, until onion softens and mixture is fragrant. Add wine; bring to the boil. Reduce heat; simmer, uncovered, 5 minutes or until liquid reduces by half.
4 Return lamb to pan with undrained apricots, stock and honey; bring to the boil. Reduce heat; simmer, covered, about 50 minutes or until lamb is tender. Remove from heat; stir in fresh coriander.
5 Divide lamb among serving plates, drizzle with yogurt and serve with couscous, if desired.

preparation time 20 minutes (plus standing time)
cooking time 1 hour **serves** 8
nutritional count per serving 10.3g total fat (3.3g saturated fat); 1689kJ (404 cal); 37.9g carbohydrate; 31.6g protein; 5.6g fibre

Curried lamb shanks

8 french-trimmed lamb shanks (2kg)
¼ cup (35g) plain flour
2 tablespoons peanut oil
1 medium brown onion (150g), chopped finely
2 cloves garlic, crushed
½ cup (150g) rogan josh curry paste
2 cups (500ml) water
400g can crushed tomatoes
1 teaspoon sugar
2 cups (500ml) beef stock
400g cauliflower, chopped coarsely
400g pumpkin, chopped coarsely
¾ cup (150g) red lentils
¼ cup coarsely chopped fresh coriander

1 Toss lamb in flour; shake away excess. Heat oil in large saucepan; cook lamb, in batches, until browned all over.
2 Cook onion and garlic in same pan, stirring, until onion softens. Add paste; cook, stirring, until fragrant. Return lamb to pan with the water, undrained tomatoes, sugar and stock; bring to the boil. Reduce heat; simmer, covered, 1½ hours.
3 Add cauliflower, pumpkin and lentils to curry; bring to the boil. Reduce heat; simmer, covered, 15 minutes or until cooked as desired. Remove from heat; stir in coriander.
4 Serve lamb with naan bread, if desired.

preparation time 20 minutes **cooking time** 2 hours 5 minutes
serves 4
nutritional count per serving 27.4g total fat (5.6g saturated fat); 3093kJ (740 cal); 37.6g carbohydrate; 78.4g protein; 13.9g fibre

pork

Italian braised pork

2 tablespoons olive oil
1.5kg pork shoulder, rolled and tied
2 cloves garlic, crushed
1 medium brown onion (150g), chopped coarsely
½ small fennel bulb (100g), chopped coarsely
8 slices hot pancetta (120g), chopped coarsely
1 tablespoon tomato paste
½ cup (125ml) dry white wine
400g can whole tomatoes
1 cup (250ml) chicken stock
1 cup (250ml) water
2 sprigs fresh rosemary
2 large fennel bulbs (1kg), halved, sliced thickly
spice rub
1 teaspoon fennel seeds
2 teaspoons dried oregano
½ teaspoon cayenne pepper
1 tablespoon cracked black pepper
1 tablespoon sea salt
2 teaspoons olive oil

1 Preheat oven to 180°C/160°C fan-forced. Heat oil in large flameproof casserole dish; cook pork, uncovered, until browned.
2 Meanwhile, combine ingredients for spice rub in small bowl.
3 Remove pork from dish; discard all but 1 tablespoon of the oil in dish. Cook garlic, onion, chopped fennel and pancetta in same dish, stirring, until onion softens. Add paste; cook, stirring, 2 minutes.
4 Meanwhile, rub pork with spice rub.
5 Return pork to dish with wine, undrained tomatoes, stock, the water and rosemary; bring to the boil. Cook, covered, in oven 1 hour. Add sliced fennel; cook, covered, in oven 1 hour.
6 Remove pork from dish; discard rind. Cover to keep warm.
7 Cook braising liquid in dish over medium heat, uncovered, until thickened slightly. Return sliced pork to dish; serve pork with sauce.

preparation time 25 minutes **cooking time** 2 hours 50 minutes
serves 6
nutritional count per serving 32.8g total fat (10.7g saturated fat); 2525kJ (604 cal); 7.5g carbohydrate; 66.5g protein; 4.6g fibre

Apples, pork and prunes

2 tablespoons vegetable oil
2 small leeks (400g), sliced thinly
800g diced pork
½ cup (75g) plain flour
1 litre (4 cups) chicken stock
½ cup (100g) white long-grain rice
4 medium apples (600g), sliced thickly
1 cup (170g) seeded prunes
2 tablespoons coarsely chopped fresh sage

1 Preheat oven to160°C/140°C fan-forced.
2 Heat half of the oil in 2.5 litre (10-cup) flameproof casserole dish; cook leek, stirring, until soft. Remove from dish.
3 Toss pork in flour; shake away excess flour.
4 Heat remaining oil in same dish; cook pork, stirring, until browned. Add leek and stock; cook, covered, in oven 45 minutes.
5 Remove dish from oven; skim off any fat. Stir in rice, apple, prunes and half of the sage; cook, covered, about 20 minutes or until pork is tender.
6 Serve sprinkled with remaining sage.

preparation time 25 minutes **cooking time** 1 hour 30 minutes
serves 4
nutritional count per serving 27.1g total fat (7.1g saturated fat); 3022kJ (723 cal); 63.9g carbohydrate; 51.4g protein; 8.3g fibre

Maple-syrup-flavoured pork belly with pecans

1kg boneless pork belly, cut into four pieces
1 cup (250ml) pure maple syrup
3 cups (750ml) chicken stock
1 cinnamon stick
2 ancho chillies
6 whole cloves
2 cloves garlic, crushed
½ cup (125ml) soy sauce
½ cup (125ml) orange juice
1 tablespoon olive oil
750g silver beet, trimmed, sliced thinly
½ cup (60g) coarsely chopped roasted pecans

1 Combine pork, syrup, stock, cinnamon, chillies, cloves, garlic and soy in saucepan large enough to hold pork in a single layer; bring to the boil. Reduce heat; simmer, covered, about 1½ hours or until pork is tender, turning pork every 30 minutes. Remove pork; cover to keep warm.
2 Stir juice into braising liquid; bring to the boil. Reduce heat; simmer, uncovered, about 5 minutes or until sauce thickens slightly. Strain sauce into small bowl.
3 Meanwhile, heat oil in large saucepan; cook silver beet, stirring, about 5 minutes or until wilted.
4 Cut each pork piece into quarters. Divide silver beet among plates; top with pork, drizzle with sauce then sprinkle with nuts. Serve with steamed basmati and wild rice blend, if desired.

preparation time 20 minutes **cooking time** 1 hour 50 minutes
serves 4
nutritional count per serving 67.2g total fat (18.9g saturated fat); 4080kJ (976 cal); 62.3g carbohydrate; 34.7g protein; 4.1g fibre

Pork green curry

800g pork mince
3cm piece fresh ginger (15g), grated
1 fresh long red chilli, chopped finely
2 cloves garlic, crushed
⅓ cup coarsely chopped fresh coriander
1 tablespoon peanut oil
¼ cup (75g) green curry paste
2 x 400ml cans coconut milk
2 tablespoons lime juice
1 tablespoon fish sauce
1 tablespoon grated palm sugar
200g snake beans, cut into 5cm lengths
⅓ cup loosely packed thai basil leaves

1 Combine pork, ginger, chilli, garlic and half the coriander in medium bowl. Roll level tablespoons of mixture into balls. Heat oil in large frying pan; cook meatballs, in batches, until browned.

2 Cook paste in same pan, stirring until fragrant. Add coconut milk; bring to the boil. Reduce heat; simmer, uncovered, stirring occasionally, about 10 minutes.

3 Return meatballs to pan with juice, sauce, sugar and beans; simmer, covered, about 5 minutes or until meatballs are cooked through. Remove from heat; stir in remaining coriander and basil off the heat. Serve with steamed jasmine rice, if desired.

preparation time 15 minutes **cooking time** 25 minutes
serves 4
nutritional count per serving 66.1g total fat (42.9g saturated fat); 3532kJ (845 cal); 13.7g carbohydrate; 47.2g protein; 7.3g fibre

Pork ragu with pappardelle

2 x 5cm-thick (750g) pork scotch steaks
2 tablespoons plain flour
1 tablespoon olive oil
20g butter, chopped
1 medium leek (350g), sliced thinly
3 cloves garlic, sliced
1 medium fennel (200g), sliced thinly
½ cup (125ml) white wine
1½ cups (375ml) chicken stock
500g pappardelle pasta
2 teaspoons balsamic vinegar
½ cup (80g) green olives
¼ cup coarsely chopped fennel fronds

1 Preheat oven to 160°C/140°C fan-forced.
2 Toss pork in flour; shake away excess flour. Heat oil and butter in a flameproof baking dish; cook pork until browned all over. Remove from dish.
3 Cook leek, garlic and fennel in same dish, stirring, until softened. Add wine; bring to the boil. Reduce heat; simmer, uncovered, until wine is almost evaporated. Add stock; bring to the boil. Return pork to dish, cover with foil; cook in oven about 2 hours or until pork is tender, turning halfway. Cool slightly and tear the pork into small pieces.
4 Meanwhile, cook pasta in large saucepan of boiling water until just tender; drain. Return to pan.
5 Reheat the pork and sauce, stir in balsamic and olives. Add pork and sauce to pasta; toss gently to combine.
6 Divide pasta among serving bowls, sprinkle with fennel fronds.

preparation time 25 minutes **cooking time** 2 hours 10 minutes
serves 6
nutritional count per serving 17.3g total fat (5.9g saturated fat); 2475kJ (592 cal); 64.6g carbohydrate; 38.1g protein; 4.8g fibre

Thai pork curry with pickled snake beans

2¾ cups (680ml) coconut milk
3⅓ cups (830ml) water
1.5kg pork shoulder, trimmed, diced into 2cm pieces
1⅔ cups (410ml) coconut cream
⅓ cup (100g) red curry paste
¼ cup (65g) grated palm sugar
¼ cup (60ml) fish sauce
6 fresh kaffir lime leaves, sliced thinly
190g can sliced bamboo shoots, drained
⅓ cup coarsely chopped fresh thai basil
¼ cup coarsely chopped fresh coriander
2 fresh long red chillies, seeded, sliced thinly
pickled snake beans
350g snake beans, cut into 5cm lengths
1 cup (250ml) water
1 cup (250ml) white vinegar
1 cup (220g) sugar
2 tablespoons salt

1 Make pickled snake beans; cover, refrigerate 3 hours before serving.
2 Bring half of the coconut milk and the water to the boil in medium saucepan. Add pork; bring to the boil. Reduce heat; simmer, uncovered, about 1 hour or until tender. Remove pan from heat; cool pork in liquid.
3 Heat coconut cream in large saucepan about 10 minutes or until fat separates from cream. Add paste; cook, stirring, 10 minutes. Stir in sugar and sauce, add 1 cup pork cooking liquid (discard the rest). Stir in remaining coconut milk, lime leaves, bamboo shoots and drained pork; simmer, uncovered, until heated through.
4 Stir basil and coriander through curry off the heat just before serving, sprinkle with chilli; serve with pickled snake beans.
pickled snake beans Place beans in medium heatproof bowl. Stir the salt, water, vinegar and sugar in small saucepan over heat until sugar dissolves; bring to the boil. Remove from heat; cool 10 minutes. Pour over beans.

preparation time 30 minutes (plus cooling and refrigeration times)
cooking time 1 hour 30 minutes **serves** 6
nutritional count per serving 63.0g total fat (40.3g saturated fat);
4381kJ (1048 cal); 57.1g carbohydrate; 60.4g protein; 7.1g fibre

Pork vindaloo

2 teaspoons cumin seeds
2 teaspoons garam masala
1 tablespoon grated fresh ginger
6 cloves garlic, crushed
8 fresh small red thai chillies, chopped finely
1 tablespoon white vinegar
1 tablespoon tamarind concentrate
1kg diced pork
2 tablespoons butter
2 large brown onions (400g), chopped coarsely
2 cinnamon sticks
6 cloves
2 teaspoons plain flour
1 litre (4 cups) beef stock
8 curry leaves
2 tablespoons finely chopped palm sugar

1 Dry-fry cumin and garam masala in large heated saucepan, stirring until fragrant; cool.
2 Combine spice mixture with ginger, garlic, chilli, vinegar, tamarind and pork in large bowl. Cover; refrigerate 1 hour.
3 Heat butter in same pan; cook onion, cinnamon and cloves, stirring, until onion is browned lightly. Add pork mixture; cook, stirring, 5 minutes or until pork is browned lightly.
4 Stir in flour. Gradually add stock and stir in leaves; simmer, covered, 30 minutes. Uncover; simmer about 30 minutes or until pork is tender and sauce thickened. Add sugar; stir until dissolved.

preparation time 15 minutes (plus refrigeration time)
cooking time 1 hour 15 minutes (plus cooling time) **serves** 6
nutritional count per serving 18.8g total fat (8.0g saturated fat); 1484kJ (355 cal); 9.3g carbohydrate; 36.7g protein; 1.6g fibre

Sausages with borlotti beans

1 tablespoon olive oil
8 thick Italian sausages (960g)
1 large brown onion (200g), chopped finely
3 cloves garlic, crushed
425g can chopped tomatoes
400g can borlotti beans, drained, rinsed
1 cup (250ml) salt-reduced beef stock
1 cup (250ml) water
2 teaspoons finely chopped fresh oregano
2 tablespoons chopped fresh flat-leaf parsley

1 Heat oil in large saucepan; cook sausages until browned. Remove sausages from pan; slice thickly.
2 Drain all but 1 tablespoon of the fat from the pan; cook onion and garlic, stirring, until onion softens. Add undrained tomatoes, beans, stock, the water and oregano.
3 Return sausages to pan; simmer, uncovered, about 10 minutes or until thickened.
4 Sprinkle sausage mixture with parsley and serve with mashed potato (see page 360), if desired.

preparation time 15 minutes **cooking time** 20 minutes
serves 4
nutritional count per serving 77.3g total fat (26.9g saturated fat); 4193kJ (1003 cal); 22.2g carbohydrate; 53.3g protein; 7.5g fibre

Pork and lemon grass curry

3 x 10cm sticks (60g) fresh lemon grass, chopped finely
4 cloves garlic, quartered
4cm piece fresh galangal (20g), sliced thinly
1 teaspoon ground turmeric
2 fresh jalapeño chillies, quartered
½ cup (125ml) water
¼ cup (60ml) peanut oil
½ teaspoon shrimp paste
2 x 400ml cans coconut milk
3 fresh kaffir lime leaves, torn
1kg pork fillet, cut into 1cm slices
2 tablespoons lime juice

1 Blend or process lemon grass, garlic, galangal, turmeric, chilli and the water until mixture forms a paste.
2 Heat 1 tablespoon of the oil in large saucepan; cook lemon grass paste and shrimp paste, stirring, about 1 minute or until fragrant. Add coconut milk and lime leaves; simmer, uncovered, about 30 minutes or until sauce thickens slightly.
3 Meanwhile, heat remaining oil in large frying pan; cook pork, in batches, until browned.
4 Add pork and juice to curry sauce; simmer, uncovered, about 2 minutes or until pork is cooked.

preparation time 20 minutes **cooking time** 45 minutes
serves 4
nutritional count per serving 75.2g total fat (45.6g saturated fat); 3925kJ (939 cal); 8.3g carbohydrate; 57.3g protein; 4.2g fibre

Braised pork with fresh sage sauce

90g butter
1.5kg rack of pork (6 cutlets)
2 medium carrots (240g), sliced thickly
6 baby onions (150g), peeled
4 cloves garlic, peeled
2 bay leaves
6 sprigs fresh thyme
1 ⅓ cups (330ml) dry white wine
fresh sage sauce
15g butter
1 tablespoon plain flour
1 tablespoon fresh sage leaves

1 Preheat oven to 160°C/140°C fan-forced.
2 Melt butter in large flameproof baking dish; cook pork until browned each side. Remove pork from dish.
3 Cook carrot, onion, garlic, bay leaves and thyme in same dish; stir over heat about 5 minutes or until just browned. Return pork to dish with wine; cook in oven about 1 ¼ hours or until tender. Remove pork; keep warm.
4 Strain cooking liquid; reserve liquid and discard vegetables. Make fresh sage sauce.
5 Serve pork with sage sauce and, if desired, roast tomatoes and potatoes.
fresh sage sauce Bring reserved liquid to the boil in medium saucepan; whisk in blended butter and flour. Boil, whisking constantly, until thickened slightly; stir in sage.

preparation time 15 minutes **cooking time** 1 hour 30 minutes
serves 6
nutritional count per serving 32.0g total fat (15.5g saturated fat); 1940kJ (464 cal); 4.3g carbohydrate; 30.9g protein; 1.6g fibre

Pork with sticky asian glaze

1 tablespoon vegetable oil
1.5kg piece pork neck
5 french shallots, sliced finely
2cm piece fresh ginger (10g), sliced finely
5 cloves garlic, sliced finely
½ cup (125ml) dark soy sauce
½ cup (100g) crushed yellow rock sugar
2 whole star anise
2 cups (500ml) chicken stock
2 cups (500ml) water
8 dried whole shiitake mushrooms
½ cup canned bamboo shoots, rinsed, drained
1kg fresh thick rice noodles
1 bunch chinese broccoli, chopped coarsely
3 green onions, sliced thinly

1 Heat oil in a large saucepan over a medium heat; cook pork until browned all over. Add shallots, ginger and garlic to pan; cook 1 minute.
2 Add soy, sugar, star anise, stock and water; bring to the boil. Reduce heat; simmer, covered, 1½ hours, turning pork occasionally.
3 Meanwhile, soak mushrooms in warm water 20 minutes. Remove stems, cut in half. Add mushrooms and bamboo shoots to pan; simmer gently, uncovered, further 30 minutes, turning pork occasionally.
4 Remove pork from pan; cover to keep warm. Strain cooking liquid into a large jug; reserve 2½ cups (625ml). Reserve mushroom mixture.
5 Bring reserved cooking liquid to the boil in medium saucepan; boil, uncovered, about 10 minutes or until reduced by half.
6 Meanwhile, place noodles in heatproof bowl; cover with boiling water. Stand until tender; drain.
7 Boil, steam or microwave broccoli until just tender. Slice pork thickly.
8 Place noodles on serving plates, top with broccoli, pork and reserved mushroom mixture. Drizzle with sauce, top with green onion.

preparation time 30 minutes (plus refrigeration time)
cooking time 2 hours 15 minutes **serves** 6
nutritional count per serving 24.3g total fat (7.3g saturated fat); 2884kJ (690 cal); 55.4g carbohydrate; 60.1g protein; 3.0g fibre

Chipotle pork ribs with chorizo and smoked paprika

4 chipotle chillies
1 cup (250ml) boiling water
1.5kg pork belly ribs
1 tablespoon olive oil
1 chorizo (170g), sliced thinly
2 medium red onions (340g), chopped coarsely
1 medium red capsicum (200g), chopped coarsely
1 medium green capsicum (200g), chopped coarsely
1 teaspoon smoked paprika
4 cloves garlic, crushed
3 x 400g cans crushed tomatoes
2 medium tomatoes (300g), chopped finely
½ cup finely chopped fresh coriander
2 teaspoons finely grated lime rind
1 clove garlic, crushed, extra

1 Preheat oven to 160°C/140°C fan-forced.
2 Soak chillies in the boiling water in small heatproof bowl 10 minutes. Discard stalks from chillies; reserve chillies and liquid.
3 Using heavy knife, separate ribs. Heat oil in large deep flameproof baking dish; cook ribs, in batches, until browned all over.
4 Cook chorizo, onion, capsicums, paprika and garlic in same dish, stirring, until onion softens. Return ribs to dish with undrained crushed tomatoes, chillies and reserved liquid. Cover; cook in oven about 1 hour. Uncover; cook in oven about 1½ hours or until ribs are tender.
5 Meanwhile, combine chopped tomato, coriander, rind and extra garlic in small bowl. Cover; refrigerate until required.
6 Top ribs with coriander mixture; serve with flour tortillas and roasted corn salsa (see page 363), if desired.

preparation time 20 minutes **cooking time** 2 hours 50 minutes
serves 4
nutritional count per serving 90.2g total fat (29.8g saturated fat); 4957kJ (1186 cal); 19.6g carbohydrate; 72.6g protein; 7.5g fibre

Pork and black-eyed beans

1 cup (200g) black-eyed beans
1kg pork neck, sliced thickly
⅓ cup (50g) plain flour
2 tablespoons olive oil
1 medium brown onion (150g), chopped coarsely
2 cloves garlic, crushed
½ teaspoon five-spice powder
1 teaspoon sichuan peppercorns, crushed coarsely
½ teaspoon chilli powder
½ cup (125ml) dry white wine
3 cups (750ml) chicken stock
2 teaspoons finely grated orange rind
½ cup coarsely chopped fresh flat-leaf parsley

1 Place beans in medium bowl, cover with cold water; stand overnight,
drain. Rinse under cold water; drain.
2 Coat pork in flour, shake away excess. Heat half the oil in large
flameproof casserole dish; cook pork, in batches, until browned all over.
3 Heat remaining oil in same dish; cook onion, garlic, five-spice, pepper
and chilli, stirring, until spices are fragrant and onion softens. Add beans,
wine and stock; bring to the boil.
4 Return pork to dish; simmer, covered, 40 minutes. Uncover; simmer
about 30 minutes or until pork is tender and sauce thickens slightly,
stirring occasionally. Remove from heat; stir in rind and parsley.

preparation time 20 minutes (plus standing time)
cooking time 1 hour 30 minutes **serves** 4
nutritional count per serving 19.9g total fat (5.1g saturated fat);
2608kJ (624 cal); 30.3g carbohydrate; 71.4g protein; 8.5g fibre

Sweet and sour tamarind pork

2 tablespoons peanut oil
4 pork forequarter chops (1kg)
1 tablespoon chinese cooking wine
1 cup (250ml) chicken stock
⅓ cup (80ml) tamarind concentrate
¼ cup (60ml) soy sauce
¼ cup (65g) grated palm sugar
1 medium red onion (170g), sliced thickly
1 medium red capsicum (200g), sliced thickly
1 medium green capsicum (200g), sliced thickly
3 green onions, sliced thickly
aromatic paste
4cm piece fresh galangal (20g), chopped finely
20cm stick fresh lemon grass (40g), chopped finely
2 cloves garlic, quartered
2 shallots (50g), chopped coarsely
1 tablespoon sambal oelek

1 Preheat oven to 150°C/130°C fan-forced.
2 Blend or process ingredients for aromatic paste until mixture becomes a thick coarse puree.
3 Heat half of the oil in large deep flameproof baking dish; cook pork, in batches, until browned both sides.
4 Heat remaining oil in same dish; cook aromatic paste, stirring, until fragrant. Return pork to dish with wine, stock, tamarind, soy, sugar, red onion and capsicums; bring to the boil. Cover; cook in oven 25 minutes, turning pork once halfway through cooking time.
5 Add green onion; cook, covered, in oven about 10 minutes or until green onion is tender. Serve with steamed rice, if desired.

preparation time 25 minutes **cooking time** 50 minutes
serves 4
nutritional count per serving 31.8g total fat (9.4g saturated fat);
2462kJ (589 cal); 26.3g carbohydrate; 42.0g protein; 2.4g fibre

Pork with beans and beer

3 cloves garlic, crushed
½ teaspoon freshly ground black pepper
1.8kg pork neck
1 tablespoon olive oil
3 rindless bacon rashers (195g), chopped finely
2 medium brown onions (300g), sliced thinly
2 teaspoons caraway seeds
375ml can beer
1 cup (200g) dried haricot beans
1½ cups (375ml) chicken stock
¼ small (300g) white cabbage, shredded finely

1 Rub combined garlic and pepper all over pork. Secure pork with string at 2cm intervals to make an even shape.
2 Heat oil in large flameproof casserole dish; cook pork until browned all over. Remove from dish.
3 Cook bacon, onion and seeds in same dish, stirring, until onion is soft and bacon browned lightly.
4 Return pork to dish with beer, beans and stock; simmer, covered, about 2 hours or until beans and pork are tender. Remove pork from dish. Add cabbage; cook, stirring, until just wilted.

preparation time 20 minutes **cooking time** 2 hours 20 minutes
serves 8
nutritional count per serving 24.4g total fat (7.8g saturated fat);
2261kJ (541 cal); 13.9g carbohydrate; 59.8g protein; 6.7g fibre

Pork and lamb cassoulet

1½ cups (300g) dried white beans
300g boned pork belly, rind removed, sliced thinly
150g piece streaky bacon, rind removed, diced into 1cm pieces
800g piece boned lamb shoulder, diced into 3cm pieces
1 large brown onion (200g), chopped finely
1 small leek (200g), sliced thinly
2 cloves garlic, crushed
3 sprigs fresh thyme
400g can crushed tomatoes
2 bay leaves
1 cup (250ml) water
1 cup (250ml) chicken stock
2 cups (140g) stale breadcrumbs
⅓ cup coarsely chopped fresh flat-leaf parsley

1 Place beans in medium bowl, cover with water; soak overnight, drain.
Rinse under cold water; drain. Place beans in medium saucepan of
boiling water; bring to the boil. Reduce heat; simmer, covered, about
15 minutes or until beans are just tender. Drain.
2 Preheat oven to 160°C/140°C fan-forced..
3 Cook pork in large flameproof casserole dish over heat, pressing down
with back of spoon on pork until browned all over; remove from dish.
4 Cook bacon in same pan, stirring, until crisp; remove from dish.
5 Cook lamb, in batches, in same pan, until browned all over.
6 Cook onion, leek and garlic in same dish, stirring, until onion softens.
Add thyme, undrained tomatoes, bay leaves, the water, stock, beans and
meat; bring to the boil. Cover; cook in oven 45 minutes. Sprinkle with
combined breadcrumbs and parsley, return to oven; cook, uncovered,
about 45 minutes or until liquid is nearly absorbed and beans are tender.

preparation time 40 minutes (plus standing time)
cooking time 2 hours 10 minutes **serves** 6
nutritional count per serving 30.1g total fat (11.3g saturated fat);
2859kJ (684 cal); 39.8g carbohydrate; 57.5g protein; 12.4g fibre

vegetables

Black bean, corn and chipotle stew

1 ½ cups (300g) dried black beans
2 chipotle chillies
½ cup (125ml) boiling water
1 tablespoon cumin seeds
2 trimmed corn cobs (500g)
2 teaspoons olive oil
1 large brown onion (200g), chopped finely
800g can crushed tomatoes
salsa
1 small red onion (100g), chopped coarsely
1 small tomato (90g), chopped coarsely
½ cup coarsely chopped fresh coriander
1 lebanese cucumber (130g), chopped coarsely
1 tablespoon olive oil
2 tablespoons lemon juice

1 Place beans in medium bowl, cover with water; stand overnight, drain. Rinse under cold water; drain. Place beans in medium saucepan of boiling water; return to the boil. Reduce heat; simmer, uncovered, about 15 minutes or until beans are just tender.
2 Preheat oven to 200°C/180°C fan-forced.
3 Place chillies and the boiling water in small bowl; stand 15 minutes. Discard stalks; blend or process chilli and its soaking liquid until smooth.
4 Meanwhile, dry-fry cumin seeds in small frying pan, stirring, until fragrant.
5 Cook corn on heated oiled grill plate (or grill or barbecue) until browned lightly and just tender. When cool enough to handle, cut kernels from cobs with sharp knife.
6 Heat oil in large flameproof dish; cook onion, stirring, until soft. Add drained beans, chilli mixture, cumin, undrained tomatoes and half of the corn; bring to the boil. Cook, uncovered, in oven about 20 minutes or until sauce thickens.
7 Combine remaining corn with salsa ingredients in medium bowl.
8 Serve stew with salsa and warmed flour tortillas, if desired.

preparation time 15 minutes (plus standing time)
cooking time 1 hour **serves** 4
nutritional count per serving 10.4g total fat (1.3g saturated fat); 1839kJ (440 cal); 61.3g carbohydrate; 26.2g protein; 19.5g fibre

Portuguese potatoes

600g sebago potatoes, chopped coarsely
2 tablespoons olive oil
1 large brown onion (200g), chopped coarsely
2 cloves garlic, crushed
4 medium tomatoes (760g), chopped coarsely
2 teaspoons sweet paprika
2 teaspoons finely chopped fresh thyme
½ cup (125ml) chicken stock
1 tablespoon piri-piri sauce
1 tablespoon coarsely chopped fresh flat-leaf parsley

1 Preheat oven to 220°C/200°C fan-forced.
2 Toss potato and half of the oil in medium shallow baking dish. Roast, uncovered, in oven about 30 minutes or until browned lightly.
3 Meanwhile, heat remaining oil in large frying pan; cook onion and garlic, stirring, until onion softens. Add tomato, paprika and thyme; cook, stirring, about 1 minute or until tomato just softens. Add stock and sauce; bring to the boil. Reduce heat; simmer, uncovered, stirring occasionally, about 10 minutes or until sauce thickens slightly.
4 Remove potato from oven; reduce oven temperature to 180°C/160°C fan-forced. Pour sauce over potato; bake, uncovered, in oven 20 minutes or until potato is tender. Serve sprinkled with parsley.

preparation time 15 minutes **cooking time** 50 minutes
serves 6
nutritional count per serving 6.5g total fat (0.9g saturated fat); 602kJ (144 cal); 15.6g carbohydrate; 4.0g protein; 3.6g fibre

Mixed mushroom ragu with polenta

50g butter
2 large brown onions (400g), chopped coarsely
3 cloves garlic, crushed
¼ cup (35g) plain flour
400g button mushrooms
400g swiss brown mushrooms, quartered
400g flat mushrooms, sliced thickly
2 tablespoons tomato paste
⅔ cup (160ml) dry red wine
2 cups (500ml) vegetable stock
2 teaspoons finely chopped fresh thyme

1 Heat butter in large saucepan; cook onion and garlic, stirring, until onion softens. Add flour; cook, stirring, until mixture bubbles. Add mushrooms; cook, stirring, until mushrooms are just tender.
2 Stir in paste and wine; bring to the boil. Reduce heat; simmer, uncovered, until liquid reduces by half. Add stock; return to the boil. Reduce heat; simmer, uncovered, 30 minutes. Stir in thyme.
3 Serve ragu on cheesy polenta (see page 367).

preparation time 20 minutes **cooking time** 50 minutes
serves 8
nutritional count per serving 6.0g total fat (3.5g saturated fat);
573kJ (137 cal); 7.5g carbohydrate; 7.6g protein; 5.0g fibre

Chickpea vegetable braise with cumin couscous

1 cup (200g) dried chickpeas
2 tablespoons olive oil
2 small leeks (400g), chopped coarsely
2 medium carrots (240g), cut into batons
2 cloves garlic, crushed
1 tablespoon finely chopped fresh rosemary
2 tablespoons white wine vinegar
2 cups (500ml) vegetable stock
100g baby spinach leaves
¼ cup (60ml) lemon juice
2 tablespoons olive oil, extra
2 cloves garlic, crushed, extra
cumin couscous
1 cup (200g) couscous
1 cup (250ml) boiling water
1 tablespoon olive oil
1 teaspoon ground cumin

1 Place chickpeas in medium bowl, cover with cold water; stand overnight, drain. Rinse under cold water; drain. Place chickpeas in medium saucepan of boiling water; return to the boil. Reduce heat; simmer, uncovered, about 40 minutes or until chickpeas are tender. Drain.
2 Meanwhile, preheat oven to 160°C/140°C fan-forced.
3 Heat oil in large deep flameproof baking dish; cook leek and carrot, stirring, until just tender. Add garlic, rosemary and chickpeas; cook, stirring, until fragrant. Add vinegar and stock; bring to the boil. Cover; cook in oven 30 minutes.
4 Meanwhile, make cumin couscous.
5 Stir spinach into dish with remaining ingredients; serve with couscous.
cumin couscous Combine couscous and the water in medium heatproof bowl, cover; stand about 5 minutes or until liquid is absorbed, fluffing with fork occasionally. Add oil and cumin; toss gently to combine.

preparation time 20 minutes (plus standing time)
cooking time 1 hour 25 minutes **serves** 4
nutritional count per serving 26.9g total fat (3.9g saturated fat); 2483kJ (594 cal); 63.2g carbohydrate; 19.0g protein; 11.4g fibre

Potato and vegetable curry

2 tablespoons vegetable oil
1 medium brown onion (150g), chopped finely
2 cloves garlic, crushed
1 tablespoon grated fresh ginger
2 fresh small red thai chillies, seeded, chopped finely
2 teaspoons ground cumin
2 teaspoons ground coriander
1 teaspoon garam masala
1 teaspoon ground turmeric
1kg potatoes, chopped coarsely
600g pumpkin, chopped coarsely
2 cups (500ml) vegetable stock
1 cup (250ml) coconut milk
200g green beans, halved
100g baby spinach leaves

1 Heat oil in large saucepan; cook onion, garlic, ginger and chilli, stirring, until onion softens. Add spices; cook, stirring, about 2 minutes or until fragrant. Add potato and pumpkin; stir to coat vegetables in spice mixture.
2 Stir in stock and coconut milk; bring to the boil. Reduce heat; simmer, covered, about 20 minutes or until potato is almost tender.
3 Stir in beans; simmer, covered, about 5 minutes or until potato is just tender. Remove from heat; stir in spinach.

preparation time 25 minutes **cooking time** 40 minutes
serves 4
nutritional count per serving 23.6g total fat (13.1g saturated fat); 1848kJ (442 cal); 41.0g carbohydrate; 12.3g protein; 8.6g fibre

Eggplant parmigiana

vegetable oil, for shallow-frying
1 medium brown onion (150g), chopped finely
2 trimmed celery stalks (200g), chopped finely
2 tablespoons brandy
2 tablespoons chopped fresh flat-leaf parsley
3 cups (750g) tomato pasta sauce
2 litres (8 cups) water
1 teaspoon sugar
2 large eggplants (1kg), sliced thickly
¾ cup (75g) packaged breadcrumbs
½ cup (40g) grated romano cheese

1 Heat 1 tablespoon of the oil in large heavy-based saucepan; cook onion and celery, stirring, until onion is soft. Add brandy and parsley; cook, stirring, until most of the brandy evaporates. Stir in pasta sauce, the water and sugar; simmer, uncovered, about 1¼ hours or until mixture thickens slightly.
2 Meanwhile, heat remaining oil in large frying pan; shallow-fry eggplant, in batches, until browned both sides. Drain on absorbent paper.
3 Preheat oven to 180°C/160°C fan-forced.
4 Place one-third of the eggplant, in single layer, in shallow 3 litre (12 cup) ovenproof dish; pour one-third of the tomato mixture over eggplant, sprinkle with half of the breadcrumbs and half of the cheese. Repeat layering, finishing with eggplant and tomato mixture.
5 Bake, uncovered, about 40 minutes or until almost set. Serve with pasta, if desired.

preparation time 35 minutes **cooking time** 2 hours 20 minutes
serves 8
nutritional count per serving 16.1g total fat (2.7g saturated fat); 1124kJ (269 cal); 20.0g carbohydrate; 5.9g protein; 5.6g fibre

Ratatouille

½ cup (125ml) olive oil
2 medium green zucchini (240g), chopped coarsely
2 medium yellow zucchini (240g), chopped coarsely
1 large eggplant (500g), chopped coarsely
1 medium red capsicum (200g), chopped coarsely
1 medium green capsicum (200g), chopped coarsely
2 medium red onions (340g), chopped coarsely
4 cloves garlic, chopped finely
800g can whole peeled tomatoes
1 fresh small red chilli
1 strip orange rind
½ teaspoon coriander seeds
2 bay leaves
1 sprig fresh basil
1 tablespoon red wine vinegar

1 Heat 1 tablespoon of the oil in large flameproof baking dish; cook zucchini, stirring, until browned. Remove from pan. Heat another tablespoon of the oil in dish; cook eggplant, stirring, until browned. Remove from pan. Repeat with another tablespoon of the oil and capsicum. Remove from pan.
2 Heat remaining 2 tablespoons of oil in large flameproof casserole dish; cook onion and garlic, stirring, until onion is soft. Add crushed tomatoes; bring to the boil. Reduce heat, simmer, uncovered, until thickened to a sauce consistency.
3 Add vegetables to dish with chilli, rind, seeds, bay leaves and basil. Simmer, covered, about 40 minutes or until vegetables are tender and mixture thickens. Stir in vinegar; remove bay leaves and rind.

preparation time 15 minutes **cooking time** 40 minutes
serves 12
nutritional count per serving 10.0g total fat (1.3g saturated fat); 543kJ (130 cal); 6.3g carbohydrate; 2.6g protein; 3.3g fibre

Okra and tomato in coconut sauce

5 cloves garlic, quartered
3 shallots (75g), chopped coarsely
2 fresh long red chillies, chopped coarsely
2 green onions, chopped finely
⅓ cup (100g) tamarind concentrate
1 tablespoon vegetable oil
400g can coconut milk
2 tablespoons lime juice
10 fresh curry leaves
500g fresh okra, halved lengthways
400g can crushed tomatoes

1 Blend or process garlic, shallots, chilli, onion and tamarind until smooth.
2 Heat oil in large saucepan; cook tamarind mixture, stirring, 2 minutes.
Add coconut milk, juice and curry leaves; simmer, uncovered, 5 minutes.
3 Add okra and undrained tomatoes; simmer, uncovered, 20 minutes or
until okra is tender.

preparation time 15 minutes **cooking time** 30 minutes
serves 4
nutritional count per serving 29.5g total fat (18.8g saturated fat);
1384kJ (331 cal); 13.4g carbohydrate; 7.6g protein; 8.9g fibre

Pumpkin and split pea tagine

1 cup (200g) green split peas
1 tablespoon olive oil
1 medium brown onion (150g), chopped finely
2 cloves garlic, crushed
2 teaspoons ground coriander
2 teaspoons ground cumin
2 teaspoons ground ginger
1 teaspoon sweet paprika
1 teaspoon ground allspice
1kg pumpkin, cut into 3cm pieces
425g can crushed tomatoes
1 cup (250ml) water
1 cup (250ml) vegetable stock
2 tablespoons honey
200g green beans, trimmed, chopped coarsely
¼ cup coarsely chopped fresh coriander

1 Cook split peas in medium saucepan of boiling water, uncovered, until just tender; drain. Rinse under cold water; drain.
2 Meanwhile, heat oil in large saucepan; cook onion, stirring, until softened. Add garlic and spices; cook, stirring, about 2 minutes or until fragrant. Add pumpkin; stir to coat in spice mixture.
3 Stir in undrained tomatoes, the water and stock; bring to the boil. Reduce heat; simmer, uncovered, about 20 minutes or until pumpkin is just tender. Stir in honey then beans and split peas, reduce heat; simmer, uncovered, about 10 minutes or until beans are just tender.
4 Remove pan from heat; stir in coriander. Serve with couscous, if desired.

preparation time 15 minutes **cooking time** 40 minutes
serves 4
nutritional count per serving 7.0g total fat (1.5g saturated fat); 1484kJ (355 cal); 54.5g carbohydrate; 19.1g protein; 11.0g fibre

Mixed dhal

2 tablespoons ghee
1 medium brown onion (150g), chopped finely
2 cloves garlic, crushed
4cm piece fresh ginger (20g), grated
1½ tablespoons black mustard seeds
1 long green chilli, chopped finely
1 tablespoon ground cumin
1 tablespoon ground coriander
2 teaspoons ground turmeric
½ cup (100g) brown lentils
⅓ cup (65g) red lentils
⅓ cup (85g) yellow split peas
⅓ cup (85g) green split peas
400g can crushed tomatoes
2 cups (500ml) vegetable stock
1½ cups (375ml) water
140ml can coconut cream

1 Heat ghee in large saucepan; cook onion, garlic and ginger, stirring, until onion softens. Add seeds, chilli and spices; cook, stirring, until fragrant.
2 Add lentils and peas to pan. Stir in undrained tomatoes, stock and the water; simmer, covered, stirring occasionally, about 1 hour or until lentils are tender.
3 Just before serving, add coconut cream; stir over low heat until dhal is heated through.

preparation time 15 minutes **cooking time** 1 hour 10 minutes
serves 4
nutritional count per serving 18.4g total fat (12.5g saturated fat); 1898kJ (454 cal); 42.6g carbohydrate; 23.3g protein; 12.7g fibre

Artichoke fricassee

1 medium lemon (140g), chopped coarsely
6 medium globe artichokes (1.2kg)
30g butter
1 medium brown onion (150g), chopped coarsely
2 cloves garlic, crushed
1 large leek (500g), sliced thickly
¼ cup (35g) plain flour
½ cup (125ml) vegetable stock
½ cup (125ml) water
1½ cups (375ml) skim milk
¾ cup (90g) frozen peas

1 Place lemon in large bowl half-filled with cold water. Discard outer leaves from artichokes; cut tips from remaining leaves, trim then peel stalks. Cut artichokes in half lengthways. Using small knife, remove and discard chokes. Place artichoke in lemon water.
2 Heat butter in large heavy-based saucepan; cook onion, garlic and leek, stirring occasionally, about 5 minutes or until vegetables just soften.
3 Add flour; cook, stirring, 1 minute. Gradually stir in stock, the water and milk, then add drained, rinsed artichokes; bring to the boil. Reduce heat; simmer, covered, about 15 minutes or until artichoke is just tender. Add peas; simmer, uncovered, until peas are heated through.

preparation time 30 minutes **cooking time** 25 minutes
serves 4
nutritional count per serving 7.4g total fat (4.3g saturated fat); 920kJ (220 cal); 22g carbohydrate; 14.7g protein; 7.1g fibre

Caponata

1 tablespoon olive oil
2 small red onions (200g), cut into 2cm pieces
1 clove garlic, chopped finely
3 trimmed celery stalks (300g), cut into 2cm pieces
2 medium red capsicums (400g), cut into 2cm pieces
2 medium tomatoes (300g), cut into 2cm pieces
cooking-oil spray
2 medium eggplants (600g), cut into 2cm pieces
½ cup (110g) white sugar
1 cup (250ml) red wine vinegar
½ cup (80g) sultanas
100g seeded black olives
⅓ cup (50g) pine nuts, roasted
1½ tablespoons drained capers, rinsed

1 Heat oil in large frying pan; cook onion, garlic, celery, capsicum and tomato, in batches, until soft. Transfer to large bowl.
2 Coat eggplant all over with oil spray; cook, in same pan, in batches, until browned. Add to capsicum mixture.
3 Cook sugar in medium frying pan over low heat, without stirring or boiling, until dissolved, swirling pan occasionally. Cook about 5 minutes or until browned lightly. Add vinegar, bring to the boil; reduce heat, simmer, uncovered, until liquid is reduced by a third. Cool to room temperature.
4 Add vinegar mixture to vegetables with remaining ingredients; stir until combined. Stand for 1 hour at room temperature before serving.

preparation time 15 minutes
cooking time 20 minutes (plus cooling and standing time) **serves** 6
nutritional count per serving 10g total fat (0.8g saturated fat);
1137kJ (272 cal); 40.6g carbohydrate; 4.9g protein; 6.1g fibre

Potato-and-olive-filled banana chillies

40g butter
2 tablespoons olive oil
3 cloves garlic, crushed
2 teaspoons ground cumin
2 teaspoons dried oregano
600g potatoes, diced into 1cm pieces
3 large tomatoes (660g), diced into 1cm pieces
1 cup (120g) seeded green olives, chopped coarsely
2 cups (240g) coarsely grated cheddar cheese
8 red or yellow banana chillies (1.3kg)
tomato sauce
1 tablespoon olive oil
1 medium red onion (170g), chopped coarsely
1 clove garlic, crushed
1 tablespoon ground cumin
2 teaspoons dried oregano
800g can diced tomatoes
½ cup (125ml) water

1 Preheat oven to 180°C/160°C fan-forced.
2 Heat butter and oil in large frying pan; cook garlic, cumin, oregano and potato, stirring occasionally, about 10 minutes or until potato is browned. Add tomato and olives; cook, stirring, about 10 minutes or until liquid has evaporated. Transfer to large bowl; stir in cheese.
3 Meanwhile, using sharp knife, make a small horizontal cut in each chilli 1cm below stem, then make lengthways slit in chilli, starting from horizontal cut and ending 1cm from tip, taking care not to cut all the way through; discard membrane and seeds. Carefully divide filling among chillies, securing each closed with a toothpick.
4 Make tomato sauce. Place chillies on tomato sauce in dish, cover; cook in oven 40 minutes or until chillies are tender. Serve with tomato sauce.
tomato sauce Heat oil in large saucepan; cook onion, garlic, cumin and oregano, stirring, until onion softens. Add undrained tomatoes and the water; bring to the boil. Reduce heat; simmer, uncovered, 10 minutes.

preparation time 50 minutes **cooking time** 1 hour 10 minutes
serves 4
nutritional count per serving 43.8g total fat (20.3g saturated fat); 2725kJ (652 cal); 39.9g carbohydrate; 24.4g protein; 11.2g fibre

Red lentil, mushroom and spinach curry

1 cup (200g) dried red lentils
1 tablespoon vegetable oil
1 teaspoon cumin seeds
1 small brown onion (80g), sliced thinly
1 clove garlic, crushed
1cm piece fresh ginger (5g), grated
2 small green chillies, sliced thinly
200g button mushrooms, halved
1½ cups (375ml) vegetable stock
½ cup (125ml) water
½ teaspoon garam masala
250g baby spinach leaves
yogurt sauce
1 cup (280g) natural yogurt
1 clove garlic, crushed
½ teaspoon salt

1 Wash lentils well under cold running water.
2 Heat oil in large frying pan; cook seeds, stirring, until fragrant. Add onion, garlic, ginger and chilli; cook, stirring, until onion softens. Add mushrooms; cook until browned lightly.
3 Add drained lentils to pan with stock and the water; bring to the boil. Reduce heat; simmer, uncovered, about 5 minutes or until lentils are tender.
4 Meanwhile, combine ingredients for yogurt sauce in small bowl.
5 Add garam masala and spinach to curry; stir until spinach has wilted.
6 Serve curry with yogurt sauce and naan bread, if desired.

preparation time 15 minutes **cooking time** 15 minutes
serves 4
nutritional count per serving 8.8g total fat (2.5g saturated fat); 1170kJ (280 cal); 24.7g carbohydrate; 20.1g protein; 10.4g fibre

Microwave chickpea and eggplant curry

1 teaspoon vegetable oil
1 large brown onion (200g), chopped finely
2 cloves garlic, crushed
1 fresh long red chilli, sliced
3cm piece fresh ginger (15g), grated
1 teaspoon ground cumin
1 teaspoon ground coriander
¼ teaspoon ground turmeric
1 small eggplant (230g), chopped coarsely
1 medium carrot (120g), chopped coarsely
1 medium green capsicum (200g), chopped coarsely
2 cups (500ml) vegetable stock
½ cup (140g) tomato paste
420g can chickpeas, rinsed, drained
¼ cup (85g) mango chutney
100g cherry tomatoes, halved
½ cup loosely packed coriander leaves

1 Combine oil, onion, garlic, chilli, ginger and spices in large microwave-safe dish. Microwave on HIGH (100%) for about 2 minutes or until onion is soft.
2 Add vegetables, stock and paste; cook, covered, on HIGH (100%) for 8 minutes, stirring halfway through cooking.
3 Add chickpeas; cook, covered, on HIGH (100%) a further 5 minutes or until vegetables are tender, stirring halfway through cooking.
4 Stir in chutney, tomatoes and coriander.
5 Serve curry with warmed chapatti or steamed rice, if desired.

preparation time 15 minutes **cooking time** 15 minutes
serves 4
nutritional count per serving 3.5g total fat (0.5g saturated fat);
773kJ (185 cal); 29.7g carbohydrate; 8.9g protein; 8.7g fibre

Chickpeas in spicy tomato sauce

¾ cup (150g) dried chickpeas
1 tablespoon olive oil
2 teaspoons cumin seeds
1 tablespoon ground coriander
¼ teaspoon cayenne pepper
1 medium brown onion (150g), chopped finely
2 cloves garlic, crushed
4cm piece fresh ginger (20g), grated
2 tablespoons tomato paste
810g can crushed tomatoes
1 cup (250ml) water
5 baby new potatoes (200g), quartered
10 baby carrots (200g), halved lengthways
½ cup coarsely chopped fresh coriander

1 Place chickpeas in medium bowl, cover with cold water; stand overnight, drain. Rinse under cold water; drain. Place chickpeas in medium saucepan of boiling water; return to the boil. Reduce heat; simmer, uncovered, about 1 hour or until tender; drain.
2 Heat oil in large saucepan; cook cumin, coriander and cayenne, stirring, until fragrant. Add onion, garlic and ginger; cook, stirring, until onion softens. Add tomato paste; cook, stirring, 2 minutes.
3 Add undrained tomatoes, the water, potato and chickpeas; bring to the boil. Reduce heat; simmer, covered, about 30 minutes, stirring occasionally, or until potato is tender and mixture has thickened.
4 Add carrot; cook, uncovered, about 5 minutes or until carrot is tender. Remove from heat; stir in coriander.

preparation time 20 minutes (plus standing time)
cooking time 1 hour 40 minutes **serves** 4
nutritional count per serving 7.4g total fat (1g saturated fat); 1062kJ (254 cal); 31.1g carbohydrate; 7.4g protein; 10.6g fibre

Black-eyed beans, okra and kumara gumbo

1 cup (200g) black-eyed beans
2 teaspoons olive oil
1 large brown onion (200g), chopped coarsely
3 cloves garlic, crushed
1 teaspoon dried thyme
2 teaspoons dried oregano
3 teaspoons ground fennel
1 teaspoon cayenne pepper
500g okra
600g kumara, chopped coarsely
2 x 425g cans crushed tomatoes
1 cup (250ml) water
1½ cups (300g) white long-grain rice
425g can baby corn, rinsed, drained

1 Place beans in medium bowl; cover with water, stand overnight, drain. Rinse under cold water; drain. Place beans in medium saucepan of boiling water; return to the boil. Reduce heat; simmer, uncovered, about 30 minutes or until beans are just tender.
2 Heat oil in large saucepan; cook onion and garlic, stirring, until onion softens. Add dried herbs and spices; cook, stirring, until fragrant.
3 Add drained beans, okra, kumara, undrained tomatoes and the water; bring to the boil. Reduce heat; simmer, uncovered, about 30 minutes or until vegetables are tender.
4 Meanwhile, cook rice in medium saucepan of boiling water, uncovered, until just tender; drain.
5 Stir corn into gumbo; cook, uncovered, until corn is heated through. Serve gumbo with rice.

preparation time 15 minutes (plus standing time)
cooking time 1 hour 15 minutes **serves** 6
nutritional count per serving 3.9g total fat (0.5g saturated fat); 1881kJ (450 cal); 83.2g carbohydrate; 20.3g protein; 15.2g fibre

Palak paneer

1 tablespoon vegetable oil
1 teaspoon cumin seeds
1 teaspoon fenugreek seeds
2 teaspoons garam masala
1 large brown onion (200g), chopped finely
1 clove garlic, crushed
1 tablespoon lemon juice
500g spinach, trimmed, chopped coarsely
¾ cup (180ml) cream
2 x 100g packets paneer cheese, cut into 2cm pieces

1 Heat oil in large frying pan; cook spices, onion and garlic, stirring, until onion softens. Add juice and half of the spinach; cook, stirring, until spinach wilts. Add remaining spinach; cook, stirring, until wilted.
2 Blend or process spinach mixture until smooth.
3 Return spinach mixture to pan; stir in cream. Add paneer; cook over low heat, uncovered, stirring occasionally, about 5 minutes or until heated through.

preparation time 10 minutes **cooking time** 20 minutes
serves 6
nutritional count per serving 24.2g total fat (14.1g saturated fat); 1124kJ (269 cal); 3.0g carbohydrate; 9.0g protein; 3.4g fibre

Vegetable tagine

20g butter
1 tablespoon olive oil
2 medium brown onions (300g), chopped coarsely
2 cloves garlic, crushed
4cm piece fresh ginger (20g), grated
2 teaspoons ground cumin
2 teaspoons ground coriander
2 teaspoons finely grated lemon rind
1kg pumpkin, chopped coarsely
400g can chopped tomatoes
2 cups (500ml) vegetable stock
400g green beans, cut into 5cm lengths
⅓ cup (55g) sultanas
1 tablespoon honey
¼ cup finely chopped fresh flat-leaf parsley
¼ cup finely chopped fresh mint

1 Heat butter and oil in large saucepan; cook onion and garlic, stirring, 5 minutes. Add ginger, spices and rind; cook, stirring, about 1 minute or until fragrant.
2 Add pumpkin, undrained tomatoes and stock; bring to the boil. Reduce heat; simmer, covered, about 15 minutes or until pumpkin is just tender. Stir in beans; cook, stirring, 5 minutes.
3 Just before serving, stir in sultanas, honey and chopped fresh herbs off the heat. Serve with couscous, if desired.

preparation time 20 minutes **cooking time** 30 minutes
serves 6
nutritional count per serving 7.1g total fat (2.8g saturated fat); 882kJ (211 cal); 26.9g carbohydrate; 7.0g protein; 5.9g fibre

Dhal with egg and eggplant

2 cups (400g) red lentils
2 teaspoons vegetable oil
1 medium brown onion (150g), chopped finely
1 clove garlic, crushed
2 teaspoons ground cumin
½ teaspoon cumin seeds
1 tablespoon tomato paste
2 cups (500ml) vegetable stock
1 litre (4 cups) water
1 large tomato (250g), chopped coarsely
3 baby eggplants (180g), chopped coarsely
4 hard-boiled eggs

1 Rinse lentils in large colander under cold water until water runs clear.
2 Heat oil in large heavy-based saucepan; cook onion, garlic, cumin, seeds and tomato paste, stirring, 5 minutes. Add lentils, stock and the water; bring to the boil. Reduce heat; simmer, uncovered, stirring occasionally, 40 minutes or until mixture thickens slightly.
3 Add tomato and eggplant to pan; simmer, uncovered, stirring occasionally, about 20 minutes or until dhal is thickened and eggplant is tender. Add whole eggs; stir gently until eggs are heated through.

preparation time 10 minutes **cooking time** 1 hour
serves 4
nutritional count per serving 10.9g total fat (2.6g saturated fat); 1698kJ (406 cal); 44.6g carbohydrate; 34.1g protein; 16.7g fibre

Mexican corn and bean stew with tortillas

2 teaspoons olive oil
1 medium green capsicum (200g), sliced thinly
1 medium brown onion (150g), sliced thinly
1 cup (165g) fresh corn kernels
3 medium tomatoes (450g), chopped coarsely
420g can kidney beans, rinsed, drained
1 fresh small red thai chilli, chopped finely
8 corn tortillas, warmed

1 Heat half of the oil in large frying pan; cook capsicum, stirring, until just tender. Remove from pan.
2 Heat remaining oil in same pan; cook onion and corn, stirring, until onion softens. Add tomato, beans and chilli; simmer, uncovered, 10 minutes.
3 Stir capsicum into tomato mixture; serve with warm tortillas.

preparation time 15 minutes **cooking time** 15 minutes
serves 4
nutritional count per serving 9.9g total fat (1.4g saturated fat);
1935kJ (463 cal); 70.3g carbohydrate; 16.6g protein; 11.5g fibre

Vegetable dhansak

1 large eggplant (500g), chopped coarsely
500g pumpkin, chopped coarsely
2 medium tomatoes (300g), peeled, chopped coarsely
1 large brown onion (200g), sliced thinly
3 cups (750ml) water
420g can chickpeas, drained, rinsed
400g can brown lentils, drained, rinsed
1 tablespoon garam masala
2 cups (400g) basmati rice
2 teaspoons vegetable oil
2 medium brown onions (300g), sliced thinly, extra
¼ cup firmly packed fresh coriander leaves
masala paste
3 dried small red chillies
2 long green chillies
2cm piece fresh ginger (10g), quartered
3 cloves garlic, quartered
½ cup loosely packed fresh coriander leaves
2 tablespoons hot water

1 Blend or process ingredients for masala paste until smooth.
2 Place eggplant, pumpkin, tomato, onion and the water in large saucepan; bring to the boil. Reduce heat; simmer, covered, 15 minutes, stirring occasionally. Drain mixture through sieve over large bowl; reserve 1½ cups of the cooking liquid, discard remainder.
3 Combine half of the chickpeas, half of the lentils and half of the vegetable mixture in another large bowl; mash lightly.
4 Dry-fry garam masala and masala paste in same cleaned pan, stirring, until fragrant. Add mashed and whole chickpeas, lentils and vegetable mixtures and reserved liquid to pan; bring to the boil. Reduce heat; simmer, uncovered, 20 minutes, stirring occasionally.
5 Meanwhile, cook rice in large saucepan of boiling water until tender; drain.
6 Heat oil in medium saucepan; cook extra onion, stirring, 10 minutes or until browned; sprinkle over dhansak. Serve with rice and lemon, if desired.

preparation time 40 minutes   **cooking time** 1 hour 30 minutes
serves 6
nutritional count per serving 3.7g total fat (0.6 saturated fat); 1614kJ (386 cal); 74.4g carbohydrate; 13.4g protein; 8.9g fibre

Italian chickpea stew

1 cup (200g) dried chickpeas
1 tablespoon olive oil
1 medium red onion (170g), chopped coarsely
2 cloves garlic, crushed
425g can chopped tomatoes
2 cups (500ml) vegetable stock
1 medium eggplant (300g), chopped coarsely
2 large zucchini (300g), chopped coarsely
2 tablespoons tomato paste
⅓ cup coarsely chopped fresh flat-leaf parsley

1 Place chickpeas in medium bowl, cover with cold water; stand overnight, drain. Rinse under cold water; drain. Place chickpeas in medium saucepan of boiling water; return to the boil. Reduce heat; simmer, uncovered, about 1 hour or until chickpeas are tender. Drain.
2 Heat oil in large saucepan; cook onion and garlic until onion softens. Add chickpeas, tomato, stock, eggplant, zucchini and tomato paste; bring to the boil. Reduce heat; simmer, covered, 30 minutes. Uncover; simmer, about 30 minutes or until mixture thickens slightly.
3 Serve stew sprinkled with parsley, and topped with grated parmesan, if desired.

preparation time 15 minutes (plus standing time)
cooking time 2 hours 10 minutes **serves** 4
nutritional count per serving 8.7g total fat (1.3g saturated fat);
1145kJ (274 cal); 29.0g carbohydrate; 13.8g protein; 12.2g fibre

Roasted root vegetable ratatouille

800g celeriac, trimmed, chopped coarsely
2 large carrots (360g), chopped coarsely
2 medium parsnips (500g), chopped coarsely
2 medium kumara (800g), chopped coarsely
⅓ cup (80ml) olive oil
1 large brown onion (200g), chopped finely
3 cloves garlic, crushed
¼ cup loosely packed fresh oregano leaves
1 tablespoon tomato paste
800g can crushed tomatoes
½ cup (125ml) dry red wine
1 cup (250ml) water
½ cup (40g) coarsely grated parmesan cheese
2½ cups (250g) coarsely grated mozzarella cheese
1 cup (70g) fresh breadcrumbs
2 teaspoons finely grated lemon rind
½ cup coarsely chopped fresh flat-leaf parsley
2 tablespoons coarsely chopped fresh oregano

1 Preheat oven to 220°C/200°C fan-forced.
2 Combine celeriac, carrot, parsnip, kumara and half of the oil in large deep baking dish. Roast, uncovered, in oven about 50 minutes or until vegetables are tender and browned lightly, stirring halfway through cooking time.
3 Meanwhile, heat remaining oil in large saucepan; cook onion, garlic and oregano leaves, stirring, until onion softens. Add tomato paste; cook, stirring, 1 minute. Add undrained tomatoes, wine and the water; bring to the boil. Boil, uncovered, 10 minutes.
4 Add tomato mixture to vegetables in dish; toss gently to combine. Sprinkle with combined cheeses, breadcrumbs, rind, parsley and chopped oregano. Cook, uncovered, in oven 20 minutes or until top is browned. Serve with a green salad, if desired.

preparation time 40 minutes   **cooking time** 1 hour 30 minutes
serves 6
nutritional count per serving 24.7g total fat (9.1g saturated fat); 2090kJ (500 cal); 43.9g carbohydrate; 22.1g protein; 12.7g fibre

on the
side

Soft polenta

3 cups (750ml) water
2 cups (500ml) vegetable stock
2 cups (340g) polenta
1 cup (250ml) milk
¼ cup (20g) finely grated parmesan cheese

1 Combine the water and stock in large saucepan; bring to the boil.
2 Gradually add polenta to liquid, stirring constantly. Reduce heat; simmer, stirring, about 10 minutes or until polenta thickens.
3 Add milk and cheese; stir until cheese melts.

preparation time 5 minutes **cooking time** 15 minutes
serves 6
nutritional count per serving 4.2g total fat (2.1g saturated fat); 1016kJ (243 cal); 41.7g carbohydrate; 8.2g protein; 1.6g fibre

Fresh peas, caraway and parmesan

You need about 1.3kg fresh peas for this recipe.

60g butter
1 teaspoon caraway seeds
2 teaspoons finely grated lemon rind
1 small red onion (100g), sliced thinly
4 cups (640g) fresh peas
⅓ cup coarsely chopped fresh flat-leaf parsley
½ cup (40g) finely grated parmesan cheese

1 Melt butter in large frying pan; cook seeds, rind and onion, stirring, until onion softens.
2 Add peas; cook, stirring, until peas are just tender. Stir in parsley; sprinkle with cheese.

preparation time 35 minutes **cooking time** 5 minutes
serves 8
nutritional count per serving 8.1g total fat (5.1g saturated fat); 598kJ (143 cal); 8.5g carbohydrate; 6.8g protein; 4.8g fibre

Celeriac mash

800g lasoda potatoes, peeled, cut into 3cm pieces
1kg celeriac, chopped coarsely
60g butter, softened
½ cup (125ml) hot cream

1 Place potato in medium saucepan with enough cold water to barely cover the potato. Boil, uncovered, over medium heat about 15 minutes or until potato is tender. Drain.
2 Meanwhile, boil, steam or microwave celeriac until tender; drain.
3 Mash potato and celeriac in large bowl; stir in butter and hot cream.

preparation time 15 minutes **cooking time** 20 minutes
serves 6
nutritional count per serving 17.6g total fat (11.4g saturated fat); 1108kJ (265 cal); 18.4g carbohydrate; 5.2g protein; 7.6g fibre

Spinach couscous

1½ cups (300g) couscous
1½ cups (375ml) boiling water
25g butter, chopped
80g finely shredded baby spinach leaves

1 Combine couscous with boiling water in large heatproof bowl, cover; stand for about 5 minutes or until water is absorbed, fluffing with fork occasionally.
2 Stir in butter and spinach.

preparation time 10 minutes (plus standing time)
serves 4
nutritional count per serving 5.6g total fat (3.5g saturated fat); 1367kJ (327 cal); 57.6g carbohydrate; 10.1g protein; 1.2g fibre

Sautéed potatoes

1kg desiree potatoes, unpeeled
2 tablespoons olive oil
50g butter, chopped

1 Cut potatoes into 1cm slices.
2 Heat oil and butter in large frying pan; cook potato, covered, over medium heat, turning occasionally, until browned lightly.
3 Reduce heat; cook, tossing pan to turn potato slices, about 10 minutes or until tender.

preparation time 5 minutes **cooking time** 20 minutes
serves 4
nutritional count per serving 19.6g total fat (8.0g saturated fat); 1425kJ (341 cal); 32.8g carbohydrate; 6.1g protein; 5.0g fibre

Spiced lentils

1½ cups (300g) red lentils
50g butter
1 small brown onion (80g), chopped finely
1 clove garlic, crushed
½ teaspoon ground coriander
½ teaspoon ground cumin
¼ teaspoon ground turmeric
¼ teaspoon cayenne pepper
½ cup (125ml) chicken stock
2 tablespoons coarsely chopped fresh flat-leaf parsley

1 Cook lentils, uncovered, in large saucepan of boiling water until just tender; drain.
2 Meanwhile, melt half of the butter in large frying pan; cook onion, garlic and spices, stirring, until onion softens.
3 Add lentils, stock and remaining butter; cook, stirring, until hot. Remove pan from heat, stir in parsley.

preparation time 5 minutes **cooking time** 15 minutes
serves 4
nutritional count per serving 11.9g total fat (7.0g saturated fat); 1354kJ (324 cal); 29.9g carbohydrate; 18.9g protein; 10.8g fibre

Garlicky beans with pine nuts

400g baby beans, trimmed
¼ cup (60ml) olive oil
1 clove garlic, sliced thinly
2 tablespoons roasted pine nuts, chopped

1 Boil, steam or microwave beans until just tender; drain. Add beans to large bowl of iced water; drain well. Place in large bowl.
2 Heat oil and garlic in small frying pan over low heat until garlic just changes colour. Add pine nuts; stir until heated through.
3 Drizzle mixture over beans.

preparation time 30 minutes **cooking time** 15 minutes
serves 4
nutritional count per serving 18.9g total fat (2.2g saturated fat);
828kJ (198 cal); 2.8g carbohydrate; 3.2g protein; 3.2g fibre

Pea mash

1kg lasoda potatoes, peeled, cut into 3cm pieces
1½ cups (180g) frozen peas
50g butter, softened
¾ cup (180ml) hot milk

1 Place potato in medium saucepan with enough cold water to barely cover the potato. Boil, uncovered, over medium heat about 15 minutes or until potato is tender. Drain.
2 Meanwhile, boil, steam or microwave peas until tender; drain. Using fork, mash peas in small bowl.
3 Mash potato in large bowl with butter and hot milk; stir in peas.

preparation time 15 minutes **cooking time** 20 minutes
serves 4
nutritional count per serving 12.4g total fat (7.9g saturated fat); 1183kJ (283 cal); 31.1g carbohydrate; 9.0g protein; 5.8g fibre

Pilaf with spinach and pine nuts

2 tablespoons olive oil
50g vermicelli noodles, broken roughly
1 cup (200g) white long-grain rice
1 small brown onion (80g), chopped finely
1 cup (250ml) vegetable stock
1½ cups (375ml) water
100g baby spinach leaves, shredded coarsely
½ cup (80g) roasted pine nuts

1 Heat oil in large saucepan with tight-fitting lid; cook vermicelli, stirring, about 2 minutes or until vermicelli is golden brown. Add rice and onion; cook, stirring, until onion softens and rice is almost translucent.
2 Add stock and the water; bring to the boil. Reduce heat; simmer, covered, about 20 minutes or until liquid is absorbed and rice is just tender.
3 Stir spinach and pine nuts into pilaf just before serving.

preparation time 10 minutes **cooking time** 25 minutes
serves 4
nutritional count per serving 23.7g total fat (2.3g saturated fat); 1789kJ (428 cal); 44.8g carbohydrate; 7.7g protein; 2.4g fibre

Mustard and honey-glazed roasted kumara

2.5kg kumara, unpeeled
⅔ cup (240g) honey
⅓ cup (95g) wholegrain mustard
2 tablespoons coarsely chopped fresh rosemary

1 Preheat oven to 220°C/200°C fan-forced.
2 Halve kumara lengthways; cut each half into 2cm wedges.
3 Combine kumara with remaining ingredients in large bowl.
4 Divide kumara mixture between two large shallow baking dishes. Roast, uncovered, about 1 hour or until kumara is tender and slightly caramelised.

preparation time 10 minutes **cooking time** 1 hour
serves 8
nutritional count per serving 0.6g total fat (0.0g saturated fat); 1229kJ (294 cal); 62.8g carbohydrate; 5.8g protein; 5.3g fibre

Mashed potato

1kg lasoda potatoes, peeled, cut into 3cm pieces
40g butter, softened
¾ cup (180ml) hot milk

1 Place potato in medium saucepan with enough cold water to barely cover the potato. Boil, uncovered, over medium heat about 15 minutes or until potato is tender. Drain.
2 Using the back of a wooden spoon, push potato through fine sieve into large bowl. Use same spoon to stir butter and hot milk into potato, folding gently until mash is smooth and fluffy.

preparation time 10 minutes **cooking time** 20 minutes
serves 4
nutritional count per serving 10.2g total fat (6.6g saturated fat); 991kJ (237 cal); 28.4g carbohydrate; 6.4g protein; 3.2g fibre

Roasted corn salsa

2 corn cobs (800g), trimmed
1 small red onion (100g), chopped coarsely
1 large avocado (320g), chopped coarsely
250g cherry tomatoes, halved
2 tablespoons lime juice
¼ cup chopped fresh coriander

1 Cook corn on heated oiled grill plate (or grill or barbecue) until browned all over. When cool enough to handle, cut kernels from cobs.
2 Combine corn kernels in medium bowl with remaining ingredients.

preparation time 15 minutes **cooking time** 15 minutes
serves 4
nutritional count per serving 14.5g total fat (2.9g saturated fat); 1200kJ (287 cal); 27.1g carbohydrate; 8.0g protein; 8.8g fibre

Pilaf with almonds

20g butter
1 clove garlic, crushed
1 cup (200g) basmati rice
1 cup (250ml) chicken stock
1 cup (250ml) water
¼ cup coarsely chopped fresh flat-leaf parsley
¼ cup (20g) roasted flaked almonds

1 Melt butter in medium saucepan; cook garlic, stirring, until fragrant.
2 Add rice; cook, stirring, 1 minute. Add stock and water; bring to the boil. Reduce heat; simmer, covered, about 20 minutes or until rice is just tender. Remove from heat; fluff rice with fork.
3 Stir in parsley and nuts.

preparation time 10 minutes **cooking time** 25 minutes
serves 4
nutritional count per serving 7.4g total fat (3.1g saturated fat); 1053kJ (252 cal); 40.3g carbohydrate; 5.2g protein; 1.2g fibre

Cheesy polenta

3 cups (750ml) water
2 cups (500ml) milk
2½ cups (250g) polenta
30g butter
½ cup (40g) finely grated parmesan cheese

1 Combine the water and milk in large saucepan; bring to the boil.
2 Gradually add polenta to liquid, stirring constantly. Reduce heat; simmer, stirring, about 10 minutes or until polenta thickens.
3 Add butter and cheese; stir until melted.

preparation time 5 minutes **cooking time** 15 minutes
serves 6
nutritional count per serving 10.4g total fat (6.3g saturated fat); 1099kJ (263 cal); 32.8g carbohydrate; 8.8g protein; 1.2g fibre

Roast potato

6 pontiac potatoes (1.3kg), halved horizontally
2 tablespoons light olive oil

1 Preheat oven to 220°C/200°C fan-forced. Oil oven tray.
2 Boil, steam or microwave potatoes 5 minutes; drain. Pat dry with absorbent paper; cool 10 minutes.
3 Gently rake rounded sides of potatoes with tines of fork; place potatoes in single layer, cut-side down, on oven tray. Brush with oil; roast, uncovered, 50 minutes or until potatoes are browned and crisp.

preparation time 10 minutes (plus cooling time)
cooking time 55 minutes **serves** 4
nutritional count per serving 9.4g total fat (1.3g saturated fat); 1062kJ (254 cal); 34.1g carbohydrate; 6.2g protein; 4.2g fibre

Spicy roasted pumpkin couscous

1 tablespoon olive oil
2 cloves garlic, crushed
1 large red onion (200g), sliced thickly
500g pumpkin, chopped coarsely
3 teaspoons ground cumin
2 teaspoons ground coriander
1 cup (200g) couscous
1 cup (250ml) boiling water
20g butter
2 tablespoons coarsely chopped fresh flat-leaf parsley

1 Preheat oven to 220°C/200°C fan-forced.
2 Heat oil in medium flameproof baking dish; cook garlic, onion and pumpkin, stirring, until vegetables are browned lightly. Add spices; cook, stirring, about 2 minutes or until fragrant.
3 Roast pumpkin mixture, uncovered, in oven, about 15 minutes or until pumpkin is just tender.
4 Meanwhile, combine couscous with the water and butter in large heatproof bowl; cover, stand about 5 minutes or until water is absorbed, fluffing with fork occasionally.
5 Add pumpkin mixture to couscous; stir in parsley.

preparation time 10 minutes **cooking time** 20 minutes
serves 4
nutritional count per serving 9.5g total fat (3.7g saturated fat); 1342kJ (321 cal); 47.8g carbohydrate; 9.4g protein; 2.7g fibre

Parsnip mash

1kg parsnip, peeled, chopped coarsely
40g butter, softened
2 cloves garlic, crushed
¾ cup (180ml) hot milk

1 Boil, steam or microwave parsnip until tender; drain.
2 Mash parsnip in large bowl with butter, garlic and hot milk.

preparation time 10 minutes **cooking time** 15 minutes
serves 4
nutritional count per serving 10.5g total fat (6.6g saturated fat);
955kJ (228 cal); 24.9g carbohydrate; 5.7g protein; 5.9g fibre

Baby carrots with orange maple syrup

1.6kg baby carrots
30g butter
2 teaspoons finely grated orange rind
2 tablespoons orange juice
2 tablespoons maple syrup

1 Boil, steam or microwave carrots until just tender; drain.
2 Melt butter in large frying pan; stir in rind, juice and maple syrup
until mixture boils. Reduce heat; simmer, uncovered, until syrup mixture
thickens slightly.
3 Add carrots; stir gently to coat in syrup mixture.

preparation time 35 minutes **cooking time** 20 minutes
serves 8
nutritional count per serving 3.3g total fat (2.0g saturated fat);
426kJ (102 cal); 14.2g carbohydrate; 1.4g protein; 5.1g fibre

Green onion couscous

1 ½ cups (300g) couscous
1 ½ cups (375ml) hot chicken stock
25g butter, chopped
3 green onions, sliced thinly

1 Combine couscous with stock in large heatproof bowl, cover; stand for about 5 minutes or until water is absorbed, fluffing with fork occasionally.
2 Stir in butter and onion.

preparation time 10 minutes (plus standing time)
serves 4
nutritional count per serving 6.0g total fat (3.6g saturated fat); 1404kJ (336 cal); 58.5g carbohydrate; 10.8g protein; 0.8g fibre

Creamed potatoes with rosemary and cheese

1kg potatoes, peeled
300ml cream
2 cloves garlic, crushed
2 chicken stock cubes, crumbled
¼ teaspoon cracked black pepper
1 tablespoon finely chopped fresh rosemary
½ cup (40g) finely grated parmesan cheese

1 Preheat oven to 180°C/160°C fan-forced. Oil shallow 2.5-litre (10-cup) ovenproof dish.
2 Using sharp knife, mandoline or V-slicer, cut potatoes into thin slices; pat dry with absorbent paper. Combine cream, garlic, stock cubes, pepper and rosemary in small bowl.
3 Layer a quarter of the potato slices, slightly overlapping, in dish; top with a quarter of the cream mixture. Continue layering with remaining potato and cream mixture.
4 Press potato firmly with spatula to completely submerge in cream mixture, cover with foil; bake 1 hour. Remove foil; sprinkle with cheese. Bake, uncovered, further 20 minutes or until potato is tender and cheese browns lightly. Stand 10 minutes before serving.

preparation time 15 minutes
cooking time 1 hour 20 minutes (plus standing time) **serves** 6
nutritional count per serving 24.1g total fat (15.7g saturated fat); 1354kJ (324 cal); 19.3g carbohydrate; 6.9g protein; 2.3g fibre

Spinach mash

1kg lasoda potatoes, cut into 3cm pieces
200g baby spinach leaves
40g butter, softened
½ cup (125ml) hot cream

1 Place potato in medium saucepan with enough cold water to barely cover the potato. Boil, uncovered, over medium heat about 15 minutes or until potato is tender; drain.
2 Meanwhile, boil, steam or microwave spinach until wilted; drain. Squeeze out excess liquid. Blend or process spinach with butter until almost smooth.
3 Mash potato in large bowl; stir in hot cream and spinach mixture.

preparation time 10 minutes **cooking time** 20 minutes
serves 4
nutritional count per serving 22.1g total fat (14.3g saturated fat); 1430kJ (342 cal); 27.5g carbohydrate; 6.7g protein; 4.6g fibre

Roasted baby vegetables

500g baby onions
250g french shallots
2 tablespoons olive oil
1kg tiny new potatoes, unpeeled
6 baby eggplants (360g), halved lengthways
250g cherry tomatoes

1 Trim off roots and remove cores of onions and shallots; discard roots and cores.
2 Preheat oven to 220°C/200°C fan-forced.
3 Heat oil in large flameproof baking dish; cook onions, shallots and potatoes, stirring, until vegetables are browned all over.
4 Roast onion mixture, uncovered, in oven, about 20 minutes or until potatoes are almost tender. Add eggplant and tomatoes; roast, uncovered, further 10 minutes or until eggplant is browned and tender.

preparation time 15 minutes **cooking time** 40 minutes
serves 4
nutritional count per serving 10.0 g total fat (1.3g saturated fat); 1308kJ (313 cal); 41.4g carbohydrate; 9.6g protein; 9.6g fibre

Risotto milanese

90g butter
1 large brown onion (200g), chopped finely
375g arborio rice
½ cup (125ml) dry white wine
3 cups (750ml) hot chicken stock
¼ teaspoon saffron powder
2 tablespoons grated parmesan cheese

1 Heat 60g of the butter in large saucepan; cook onion, stirring, until onion softens. Add rice; stir to coat in butter mixture.
2 Stir in wine, 1 cup of the stock and saffron; bring to the boil. When liquid is almost absorbed, stir in another 1 cup of the stock; return to the boil. When liquid is almost absorbed, stir in remaining stock; reduce heat. Cook until stock is absorbed. Total cooking time should be about 30 minutes or until rice is tender.
3 Stir in remaining butter and cheese until butter melts.

preparation time 15 minutes **cooking time** 40 minutes
serves 6
nutritional count per serving 13.9g total fat (8.9g saturated fat); 1580kJ (378 cal); 52.2g carbohydrate; 7.0g protein; 0.9g fibre

Warm bean and lentil salad

⅔ cup (130g) french-style green lentils
500g baby green beans, trimmed
2 medium tomatoes (240g), seeded, chopped
¼ cup finely chopped fresh chives
vinaigrette
1 shallot, chopped finely
1 tablespoon dijon mustard
2 tablespoons white wine vinegar
2 tablespoons olive oil

1 Cook lentils, uncovered, in medium saucepan of boiling water about 15 minutes or until just tender; drain.
2 Meanwhile, make vinaigrette.
3 Boil, steam or microwave beans until just tender; drain.
4 Place lentils and beans in medium bowl with tomato, chives and vinaigrette; toss gently to combine.
vinaigrette Combine shallot, mustard and vinegar in small bowl. Gradually add oil, whisking to combine.

preparation time 20 minutes **cooking time** 20 minutes
serves 8
nutritional count per serving 5.1g total fat (0.7g saturated fat); 468kJ (112 cal); 8.5g carbohydrate; 5.8g protein; 4.4g fibre

allspice also called pimento or jamaican pepper; so-named as it tastes like a combination of nutmeg, cumin, clove and cinnamon. Available whole or ground.

almonds

blanched brown skins removed.

slivered small pieces cut lengthways.

artichokes

globe large flower-bud of a member of the thistle family; it has tough petal-like leaves, and is edible in part when cooked.

hearts tender centre of the globe artichoke. Buy from delicatessens or canned in brine.

bacon rashers also called bacon slices.

barley, pearl has had the husk removed then hulled and polished so that only the "pearl" of the original grain remains, much the same as white rice.

beans

black-eyed also called black-eyed peas; the dried seed of a variant of the snake or yard-long bean. Not too dissimilar to white beans in flavour.

broad also called fava, windsor and horse beans; available dried, fresh, canned and frozen. Fresh and frozen forms should be peeled twice before use.

cannellini similar in appearance and flavour to other white beans

such as haricot, navy and great northern. Available dried or canned.

haricot similar in flavour and appearance to other small dried white beans such as great northern, navy and cannellini.

kidney medium-sized red bean, slightly floury in texture yet sweet in flavour. Available dried or canned.

lima large, flat kidney-shaped, beige dried and canned beans. Also known as butter beans.

mexican-style a mildly spiced canned combination of red kidney or pinto beans, capsicum and tomato.

snake long (about 40cm), thin, round, fresh green bean, Asian in origin; similar in taste to green or french beans.

beetroot also known as beets.

breadcrumbs

fresh bread, often white, processed into crumbs.

packaged prepared fine-textured, crunchy white breadcrumbs.

stale crumbs made by grating, blending or processing 1- or 2-day-old bread.

broccolini a cross between broccoli and chinese kale; long asparagus-like stems with a long loose floret, both completely edible. Resembles broccoli, but is milder and sweeter.

buk choy also known as bok choy, pak choi, chinese white cabbage or chinese chard; has a fresh, mild mustard taste. Use both stems and leaves. Baby buk choy, also known as pak kat farang or shanghai bok choy, is much smaller and more tender.

butter we use salted butter unless stated otherwise.

buttermilk in spite of its name, it is actually low in fat. Originally the term given to the slightly sour liquid left after butter was churned from cream, today it is intentionally made from no-fat or low-fat milk to which specific bacterial cultures have been added during the manufacturing process. Available from the dairy department in supermarkets.

capers sold dried and salted or pickled in a vinegar brine; baby capers are also available, both in brine or dried in salt.

capsicum also known as pepper or bell pepper.

cardamom native to India and used extensively in its cuisine; available in pod, seed or ground form. Has a distinctive aromatic, sweetly rich flavour and is one of the world's most expensive spices.

cashews plump, kidney-shaped, golden-brown nuts with a

distinct sweet, buttery flavour. They contain about 48 per cent fat, so should be kept, sealed tightly, under refrigeration to avoid becoming rancid. We use roasted unsalted cashews in this book, unless otherwise stated.

cayenne pepper is a thin-fleshed, long, extremely hot, dried red chilli, usually ground.

celeriac tuberous root with knobbly brown skin, white flesh and a celery-like flavour. Keep peeled celeriac in acidulated water to stop it from discolouring before use.

cheese

fetta Greek in origin; a crumbly textured goat- or sheep-milk cheese having a sharp, salty taste. Ripened and stored in salted whey.

mozzarella soft, spun-curd cheese traditionally made from water-buffalo milk. Now generally manufactured from cow milk, it is the most popular pizza cheese because of its low melting point and elasticity when heated (used for texture rather than flavour).

paneer a simple, delicate fresh cheese used in Indian dishes; substitute with ricotta.

parmesan also called parmigiano, parmesan is a hard, grainy cow-milk cheese which originated in the Parma region of Italy. The curd for this cheese is salted in brine for a month before being aged for up to 2 years, preferably in humid conditions.

ricotta a soft, sweet, moist, white cow-milk cheese with a low fat content (about 8.5%) and a slightly grainy texture.

chickpeas also known as garbanzos.

chilli use rubber gloves when seeding and chopping fresh chillies as they can burn your skin. We use seeded chillies in our recipes as the seeds contain the heat; use fewer chillies rather than seeding the lot.

ancho mild, dried chillies commonly used in Mexican cooking.

chipotle pronounced cheh-pote-lay. The name used for jalapeño chillies once they've been dried and smoked. Having a deep, intensely smokey flavour, rather than a searing heat, chipotles are dark brown, almost black in colour and wrinkled in appearance.

jalapeño pronounced hah-lah-pain-yo. Fairly hot, medium-sized, plump, dark green chilli; available pickled, sold canned or bottled, and fresh, from greengrocers.

red thai also called "scuds"; tiny and very hot.

chinese cooking wine also called shao hsing or chinese rice wine; made from fermented rice, wheat, sugar and salt with a 13.5 per cent alcohol content. Inexpensive and found in Asian food shops; if you can't find it, replace with mirin or sherry.

chorizo sausage of Spanish origin, made of coarsely ground pork and highly seasoned with garlic and chilli.

choy sum also called pakaukeo or flowering cabbage, a member of the buk choy family. Has long stems, light green leaves and yellow flowers; both stems and leaves are edible.

cinnamon available as sticks (quills) and ground into powder; one of the world's most common spices, used universally as a sweet, fragrant flavouring in both sweet and savoury dishes.

cloves dried flower buds of a tropical tree; can be used whole or in ground form. They have a strong scent and taste so should be used sparingly.

coconut

cream obtained from the first pressing of the coconut flesh alone, without the addition of water. Available in cans and cartons at most supermarkets.

flakes dried flaked coconut flesh.

milk not the liquid inside the fruit (coconut water), but the diluted liquid from the second pressing of the white flesh of a mature coconut. Available in cans and cartons at most supermarkets.

coriander also known as cilantro, pak chee or chinese parsley; bright-green-leafed herb with a pungent aroma and taste. Coriander seeds are dried and sold whole or ground, and neither form tastes remotely like the fresh leaf.

cornflour also called cornstarch. Made from corn or wheat.

couscous a fine, grain-like cereal product made from semolina; from the countries of North Africa. It is rehydrated by steaming or with the addition of a warm liquid and swells to three or four times its original size.

cumin also called zeera or comino and resembles caraway in size; is the dried seed of a plant related to the parsley family.

currants dried tiny, almost black raisins so-named from the grape type native to Corinth, Greece. These are not the same as fresh currants, which are the fruit of a plant in the gooseberry family.

dashi the basic fish and seaweed stock that accounts for the distinctive flavour of many Japanese dishes. Made from dried bonito (a type of tuna) flakes and kombu (kelp); instant dashi (dashi-no-moto) is available in powder, granules and liquid concentrate from Asian food shops.

eggplant also known as aubergine.

fennel also known as finocchio or anise; a crunchy green vegetable slightly resembling celery. Also the name given to the dried seeds of the plant which have a stronger licorice flavour.

fenugreek hard, dried seed usually sold ground as an astringent spice powder.

fish sauce called naam pla (Thai) or nuoc naam (Vietnamese); the two are almost identical. Made from pulverised salted fermented fish (most often anchovies); has a pungent smell and strong taste. Available in varying degrees of intensity, so use according to your taste.

five-spice powder ingredients may vary, but is most often a mixture of ground cinnamon, cloves, star anise, sichuan pepper and fennel seeds.

flour, plain also called all-purpose flour.

gai lan also known as gai larn, chinese broccoli and chinese kale; green vegetable appreciated more for its stems than its coarse leaves.

galangal also known as ka or lengkaus if fresh and laos if dried and powdered; a root, similar to ginger in its use. It has a hot-sour ginger-citrusy flavour.

garam masala literally meaning blended spices in its northern Indian place of origin; based on varying proportions of cardamom, cinnamon, cloves, coriander, fennel and cumin, roasted and ground together.

ghee clarified butter; with milk solids removed, this fat can be heated to a high temperature without burning.

ginger
fresh also known as green or root ginger; the thick gnarled root of a tropical plant.

ground also known as powdered ginger.

hoisin sauce a thick, sweet and spicy Chinese barbecue sauce made from salted fermented soybeans, onions and garlic; used as a marinade or baste, or to accent stir-fries and barbecued or roasted foods. From Asian food shops and supermarkets.

horseradish cream a commercial paste made of grated horseradish, vinegar, oil and sugar.

kaffir lime leaves also called bai magrood; looks like two glossy dark green leaves joined end to end, forming a rounded hourglass shape. Used fresh or dried in many South East Asian dishes, they are used like bay leaves. Sold fresh, dried or frozen, dried leaves are less potent so double the number if using as a substitute for fresh; a strip of fresh lime peel may be substituted for each kaffir lime leaf.

kecap manis a dark, thick sweet soy sauce.

kumara the polynesian name of an orange-fleshed sweet potato often confused with yam.

lemon grass a tall, clumping, lemon-smelling and tasting, sharp-edged aromatic tropical grass; the white lower part of the stem is used.

lentils (red, brown, yellow) dried pulses often identified by and named after their colour. Eaten by cultures all over the world, most famously perhaps in the dhals of India, lentils have a high food value.

maple syrup distilled from the sap of maple trees found only in Canada and parts of North America. Maple-flavoured syrup or pancake syrup is not an adequate substitute for the real thing.

merguez sausages a small, spicy sausage believed to have originated in Tunisia but eaten throughout North Africa, France and Spain, merguez is traditionally made with lamb meat and is easily recognised because of its chilli-red colour. Can be fried, grilled or roasted; available from many butchers and delicatessens.

mirin a Japanese champagne-coloured cooking wine, made of glutinous rice and alcohol. Used expressly for cooking, it should not be confused with sake. A seasoned sweet mirin, manjo mirin, made of water, rice, corn syrup and alcohol, is used in Japanese dipping sauces.

mushrooms

button small, cultivated white mushrooms with a mild flavour.

shiitake *fresh*, are also called chinese black, forest or golden oak mushrooms. Although cultivated, they have the earthiness and taste of wild mushrooms. Large and meaty, they can be used as a substitute for meat in some Asian vegetarian dishes. *Dried*, are called as donko or dried chinese mushrooms; have a unique meaty flavour. Rehydrate before use.

swiss brown also known as roman or cremini. Light to dark brown mushrooms with full-bodied flavour; suited for use in casseroles or being stuffed and baked.

mustard

black seeds also called brown mustard seeds; they are more pungent than the white variety.

dijon also called french; is a pale brown, creamy, distinctively flavoured, fairly mild French mustard.

wholegrain also called seeded. A French-style coarse-grain mustard made from crushed mustard seeds and dijon-style french mustard.

noodles

buckwheat also known as soba, there are a myriad different varieties made of a combination of buckwheat and varying proportions of wheat flour.

udon available fresh and dried, these broad, white, wheat Japanese noodles are similar to the ones in home-made chicken noodle soup.

oil

olive made from ripened olives. Extra virgin and virgin are from the first and second press, respectively, and are therefore considered the best; those labelled "extra light" or "light" refer to taste not fat levels.

peanut pressed from ground peanuts; most commonly used oil in Asian cooking because of its capacity to handle high heat without burning.

vegetable a number of oils sourced from plant rather than animal fats.

okra also called bamia or lady fingers. A green, ridged, oblong pod with a furry skin. Native to Africa, this vegetable is used in Indian, Middle Eastern and South American cooking; can be eaten on its own, in casseroles, or can be used to thicken stews.

onion

green also known as scallion or (incorrectly) shallot; an immature onion picked before the bulb has formed, having a long, bright-green edible stalk.

shallots also called french shallots, golden shallots or eschalots. Small, elongated, brown-skinned member of the onion family; they grow in tight clusters similar to garlic.

spring crisp, narrow green-leafed tops and a round sweet white bulb larger than green onions.

orange flower water concentrated flavouring made from orange blossoms.

oyster sauce Asian in origin, this thick, richly flavoured brown sauce is made from oysters and their brine, cooked with salt and soy sauce, and thickened with starches.

pancetta an Italian unsmoked bacon, pork belly cured in salt and spices then rolled into a sausage shape and dried for several weeks. Used, sliced or chopped,

as an ingredient rather than eaten on its own.

paprika ground dried sweet red capsicum (bell pepper); there are many grades and types available, such as sweet, hot, mild and smoked.

pine nuts also known as pignoli; not in fact a nut but a small, cream-coloured kernel from pine cones. They are best roasted before use to bring out the flavour.

piri-piri sauce a Portuguese chilli paste made from red chillies, ginger, garlic, oil and various herbs.

polenta also called cornmeal; a flour-like cereal made of dried corn (maize). Also the name of the dish made from it.

potatoes

baby new also called chats; not a separate variety but an early harvest with very thin skin. Good unpeeled steamed, eaten hot or cold in salads.

desiree oval, smooth and pink-skinned, waxy yellow flesh; good in salads, boiled and roasted.

lasoda round, red skin with deep eyes, white flesh; good for mashing or roasting.

pontiac large, red skin, deep eyes, white flesh; good grated, boiled and baked.

sebago white skin, oval; good fried, mashed and baked.

preserved lemon whole or quartered salted lemons preserved in a mixture of olive oil and lemon juice are a North African specialty, usually added to casseroles and tagines to impart a rich, salty-sour acidic flavour. Available from specialty food shops and delicatessens. Rinse well under cold water before using.

prosciutto a kind of unsmoked Italian ham; salted, air-cured and aged, it is usually eaten uncooked.

quince yellow-skinned fruit with hard texture and astringent, tart taste; eaten cooked or as a preserve. Long, slow cooking makes the flesh a deep rose pink.

rice

basmati a white, fragrant long-grained rice, the grains fluff up when cooked; wash several times before cooking.

jasmine or Thai jasmine, is a long-grained white rice with a perfumed aromatic quality; moist in texture, it clings together after cooking.

koshihikari small, round-grain white rice. Substitute white short-grain rice and cook by the absorption method.

risoni small rice-shape pasta; very similar to orzo.

saffron stigma of a member of the crocus family, available ground or in strands; imparts a yellow-orange colour to food once infused. The quality can vary greatly; the best is the most expensive spice in the world.

sambal oelek also ulek or olek; Indonesian in origin, this is a salty paste made from ground chillies and vinegar.

sesame seeds black and white are the most common of this small oval seed, however there are also red and brown varieties. A good source of calcium, the seeds are used in cuisines the world over as an ingredient and as a condiment. To toast, spread the seeds in a heavy-base frying pan; toast briefly over low heat.

shrimp paste also called kapi, trasi and blanchan; a strong-scented, very firm preserved paste made of salted dried shrimp. Used sparingly as a pungent flavouring, it should be chopped or sliced thinly then wrapped in foil and roasted before use.

sichuan peppercorns also called szechuan or chinese pepper; a mildly hot spice. While not related to the peppercorn family, its small, red-brown aromatic berries do look like black peppercorns and have a distinctive peppery-lemon flavour and aroma.

silver beet also known as swiss chard and incorrectly, spinach; has fleshy stalks and large leaves.

soy sauce also called sieu; made from fermented soybeans. Several varieties are available in supermarkets and Asian food stores; we use Japanese soy sauce unless stated otherwise.

spatchcock a small chicken (poussin), no more than 6 weeks old, weighing a maximum of 500g. Also, a cooking term to describe splitting a small chicken open, then flattening and grilling.

spinach also known as english spinach and, incorrectly, silverbeet. Baby spinach leaves are eaten raw in salads; larger leaves can be cooked until just wilted.

star anise a dried star-shaped pod; its seeds have an astringent aniseed flavour.

sugar

brown extremely soft, fine granulated sugar retaining molasses for its characteristic colour and flavour.

palm also called nam tan pip, jaggery, jawa or gula melaka; made from the sap of the sugar palm tree. Light brown to black in colour and usually sold in rock-hard cakes; use brown sugar if unavailable.

tamarind the tamarind tree produces clusters of hairy brown pods, each of which is filled with seeds and a viscous pulp, that are dried and pressed into the blocks of tamarind found in Asian food shops. Has a sweet-sour, slightly astringent taste.

concentrate the commercial result of the distillation of tamarind juice into a condensed, compacted paste.

turmeric also called kamin; a rhizome related to galangal and ginger. Must be grated or pounded to release its acrid aroma and pungent flavour. Known for the golden colour it imparts, fresh turmeric can be substituted with the more common dried powder.

vinegar, balsamic originally from Modena, Italy, there are now many balsamic vinegars on the market ranging in pungency and quality depending on how, and for how long, they have been aged. Quality can be determined up to a point by price; use the most expensive sparingly.

worcestershire sauce thin, dark-brown spicy sauce developed by the British when in India.

yogurt we use plain full-cream yogurt unless stated otherwise.

zucchini also known as courgette.

index

MEASURES

One Australian metric measuring cup holds approximately 250ml, one Australian metric tablespoon holds 20ml, one Australian metric teaspoon holds 5ml.

The difference between one country's measuring cups and another's is within a two- or three-teaspoon variance, and will not affect your cooking results. North America, New Zealand and the United Kingdom use a 15ml tablespoon.

All cup and spoon measurements are level. The most accurate way of measuring dry ingredients is to weigh them. When measuring liquids, use a clear glass or plastic jug with the metric markings.

We use large eggs with an average weight of 60g.

LIQUID MEASURES

METRIC	IMPERIAL
30ml	1 fluid oz
60ml	2 fluid oz
100ml	3 fluid oz
125ml	4 fluid oz
150ml	5 fluid oz (¼ pint/1 gill)
190ml	6 fluid oz
250ml	8 fluid oz
300ml	10 fluid oz (½ pint)
500ml	16 fluid oz
600ml	20 fluid oz (1 pint)
1000ml (1 litre)	1¾ pints

LENGTH MEASURES

METRIC	IMPERIAL
3mm	⅛in
6mm	¼in
1cm	½in
2cm	¾in
2.5cm	1in
5cm	2in
6cm	2½in
8cm	3in
10cm	4in
13cm	5in
15cm	6in
18cm	7in
20cm	8in
23cm	9in
25cm	10in
28cm	11in
30cm	12in (1ft)

DRY MEASURES

METRIC	IMPERIAL
15g	½oz
30g	1oz
60g	2oz
90g	3oz
125g	4oz (¼lb)
155g	5oz
185g	6oz
220g	7oz
250g	8oz (½lb)
280g	9oz
315g	10oz
345g	11oz
375g	12oz (¾lb)
410g	13oz
440g	14oz
470g	15oz
500g	16oz (1lb)
750g	24oz (1½lb)
1kg	32oz (2lb)

OVEN TEMPERATURES

These oven temperatures are only a guide for conventional ovens.
For fan-forced ovens, check the manufacturer's manual.

	°C (CELSIUS)	°F (FAHRENHEIT)	GAS MARK
Very slow	120	250	½
Slow	150	275 – 300	1 – 2
Moderately slow	160	325	3
Moderate	180	350 – 375	4 – 5
Moderately hot	200	400	6
Hot	220	425 – 450	7 – 8
Very hot	240	475	9

399

General manager Christine Whiston
Editorial director Susan Tomnay
Creative director Hieu Chi Nguyen
Editor Stephanie Kistner
Designer Caryl Wiggins
Food director Pamela Clark
Food editor Cathie Lonnie
Associate food editor Alex Somerville
Nutritional information Rebecca Squadrito
Director of sales Brian Cearnes
Marketing manager Bridget Cody
Business analyst Ashley Davies
Operations manager David Scotto
International rights enquires Laura Bamford
lbamford@acpuk.com

ACP Books are published by ACP Magazines
a division of PBL Media Pty Limited
Group publisher, Women's lifestyle Pat Ingram
Director of sales, Women's lifestyle Lynette Phillips
Commercial manager, Women's lifestyle Seymour Cohen
Marketing director, Women's lifestyle Matthew Dominello
Public relations manager, Women's lifestyle Hannah Deveraux
Creative director, Events, Women's lifestyle Luke Bonnano
Research Director, Women's lifestyle Justin Stone
ACP Magazines, Chief Executive officer Scott Lorson
PBL Media, Chief Executive officer Ian Law

Produced by ACP Books, Sydney.
Published by ACP Books, a division of ACP Magazines Ltd.
54 Park St, Sydney NSW Australia 2000. GPO Box 4088, Sydney, NSW 2001.
Phone +61 2 9282 8618 Fax +61 2 9267 9438
acpbooks@acpmagazines.com.au www.acpbooks.com.au
Printed by Toppan Printing Co., China.

Australia Distributed by Network Services, GPO Box 4088, Sydney, NSW 2001.
Phone +61 2 9282 8777 Fax +61 2 9264 3278 networkweb@networkservicescompany.com.au
United Kingdom Distributed by Australian Consolidated Press (UK),
10 Scirocco Close, Moulton Park Office Village, Northampton, NN3 6AP.
Phone +44 1604 642 200 Fax +44 1604 642 300
books@acpuk.com www.acpuk.com
New Zealand Distributed by Netlink Distribution Company, ACP Media Centre, Cnr Fanshawe
and Beaumont Streets, Westhaven, Auckland. PO Box 47906, Ponsonby, Auckland, NZ.
Phone +64 9 366 9966 Fax 0800 277 412 ask@ndc.co.nz
South Africa Distributed by PSD Promotions, 30 Diesel Road Isando, Gauteng Johannesburg.
PO Box 1175, Isando 1600, Gauteng Johannesburg.
Phone +27 11 392 6065/6/7 Fax +27 11 392 6079/80 orders@psdprom.co.za

Clark, Pamela.
The Australian women's weekly stew.
Includes index.
ISBN 978-1-86396-754-9 (pbk)
1. Stews.
I. Clark, Pamela.
641.823
© ACP Magazines Ltd 2008
ABN 18 053 273 546
This publication is copyright. No part of it may be reproduced or
transmitted in any form without the written permission of the publishers.

To order books, phone 136 116 (within Australia).
Send recipe enquiries to: recipeenquiries@acpmagazines.com.au

Cover Beef and onion casserole, p125
Photographer Tanya Zouev
Stylist Jane Hann
Food preparation Ariarne Bradshaw
Illustrations Hannah Blackmore
Acknowledgments Wheel & Barrow